BURNING TONGUES

Aleš Šteger was born in 1973 in Ptuj, Slovenia – where he grew up – then part of the former Yugoslavia ruled by Tito, which gained its independence when he was 18. He published his first collection in 1995 at the age of 22, and was immediately recognised as a key voice in the new generation of post-Communist poets not only in Slovenia but throughout central Europe.

He has published nine books of poetry, three novels and two books of essays. A Chevalier des Artes et Lettres in France and a member of the Berlin Academy of Arts, he received the 1998 Veronika Prize for the best Slovenian poetry book, the 1999 Petrarch Prize for young European authors, the 2007 Rožanc Award for the best Slovenian book of essays, the 2016 International Bienek Prize and the 2022 International Spycher Prize. His work has been translated into over 15 languages, including Chinese, German, Czech, Croatian, Hungarian, and Spanish.

Six of his books have been published in English: *The Book of Things* (BOA Editions, US, 2010), which won the 2011 Best Translated Book Award and the 2011 Best Literary Translation into English Award from AATSEEL; the collection of lyric essays *Berlin* (Counterpath, US, 2015); the book of prose poems *Essential Baggage* (Equipage, 2016); the novel *Absolution* (Istros Books, 2017); *Above the Sky Beneath the Earth* (White Pine Press, US, 2019); and *The Book of Bodies* (White Pine Press, US, 2022). His retrospective, *Burning Tongues: New & Selected Poems*, was published by Bloodaxe Books in the UK in 2022.

He studied philosophy, comparative literature and German, and edits philosophy titles for Beletrina. He has also worked in the field of visual arts (most recently with a large-scale installation at the International Kochi-Muziris Biennale in India), completed several collaborations with musicians and composers including Jure Tori and Vito Žuraj, and collaborated with Peter Zach on the film *Beyond Boundaries*.

Aleš Šteger

BURNING TONGUES

NEW & SELECTED POEMS

EDITED & TRANSLATED BY

BRIAN HENRY

BLOODAXE BOOKS

ISBN: 978 1 78037 625 7

First published 2022 by
Bloodaxe Books Ltd,
Eastburn,
South Park,
Hexham,
Northumberland NE46 1BS.

www.bloodaxebooks.com
For further information about Bloodaxe titles
please visit our website and join our mailing list
or write to the above address for a catalogue.

Supported using public funding by
ARTS COUNCIL
ENGLAND

Thanks are due to the Slovenian Book Agency/
Javna agencija za knjigo Republike Slovenije (JAK)
for its support, including grants for translation costs
for individual books covered by this selection.

JAK SLOVENIAN
BOOK
AGENCY

Cover design: Neil Astley & Pamela Robertson-Pearce.

Printed in Great Britain by Bell & Bain Limited, Glasgow, Scotland, on
acid-free paper sourced from mills with FSC chain of custody certification.

CONTENTS

from **THE BOOK OF BODIES** (2010)

from **ABOVE THE SKY BENEATH THE EARTH** (2015)

from TESTIMONY (2020)

NEW POEMS

TRANSLATOR'S NOTE

I first met Aleš Šteger in 1999 at the Days of Poetry and Wine Festival in Medana, a Slovenian village on the Italian border. Thanks to a recommendation by Tomaž Šalamun, I'd been invited to read at the festival, which Šteger founded in 1996. While Slovenian poetry was already important to me, spending time in Slovenia and meeting Šteger and other Slovenian poets turned it into something of a preoccupation. A few years later, I started translating Slovenian poetry, beginning with Šalamun's *Woods and Chalices*. In 2006, when I went to Lipica, Slovenia to participate in the Vilenica International Literary Festival, I met with Šalamun to discuss the manuscript. I expressed surprise that none of Šteger's books had been translated into English yet and asked Šalamun which book I should start with if I wanted to translate Šteger's poetry. He immediately suggested *The Book of Things*, which had appeared in Slovenia the year before. A few days later, at a café in Ljubljana, I began to translate 'A', the first poem in that collection. Since that day, I have translated a few hundred of Šteger's poems.

With my Šteger translations, I strive for accuracy while keeping in mind the need to create parallel primary texts that work as poems in English. This doesn't mean that I want my translations to read as if they'd been written in English; on the contrary, I feel that it's important for a translated poem to maintain stylistic aspects of the original even if doing so resists quick comprehension. As a translator, I'm constantly aware of the pitfalls of clarification and over-interpretation, which can dispel the mystery or ambiguity of the original in the pursuit of accessibility. Because these are poems, not technical instructions or newspaper articles, I view mystery, paradox and ambiguity as features to be retained, even embraced. While I might alter the syntax of the original in order to avoid unnecessary awkwardness or confusion in the translation, I maintain stanza structures, line logic and repetition as well as idiosyncrasies of punctuation (such as the use of commas where full stops would more commonly be used, or the absence of commas where they'd usually appear) and syntactical constructions that seem slightly peculiar or unfamiliar in English. I aim for a middle ground between domestication and foreignisation, where a poem in English not only emerges from a poem in Slovenian, but also reflects and, I hope, honours the original.

While translating, I view a poem as a sonic scaffolding where certain moments in the architecture of the original poem (such as alliteration, assonance or internal rhyme) don't always match those corresponding moments in the translation but are compensated for somewhere else in the poem. I also work to retain the formal and stylistic integrity of the original, which seems especially important for poems with unusually long sentences and poems such as 'The word ____' poems from *The Book of Bodies*, whose verticality, unconventional syntax and wordplay are as integral to the poems as their meaning. Although I use my experience as a poet when I translate, I'm careful not to impose my own aesthetic preferences on my translations. If a poet-translator attempts to align everything they translate with their own poetics, they risk producing translations that sound like their own poems. While a resolutely literal translation of a poem might sound more like an artefact than a poem, a translation that takes too many liberties or over-embellishes the original can sound like an entirely new, different poem, essentially becoming more imitation than translation. If I deviate from the original (say, by changing a word in order to adhere to a formal constraint in the original), I check with Šteger to make sure that the change is justified.

Whenever I'm in Slovenia, I meet with Šteger to discuss my translations of his work. While he can answer my questions about certain phrases, neologisms, references or allusions over email, being together allows us to gauge the lyric compatibility of the original poems and the translations. Šteger will read his poem in Slovenian, then I will read my translation, and we'll compare rhythm, duration, pace, lyricism and tone to make sure that the translations embody the poetic qualities of the original poems. This process makes translation feel less like solitary work and more like a collaboration. *Burning Tongues: New & Selected Poems* is the fruit of that collaboration.

BRIAN HENRY
July 2022

Kashmir

(1995)

About the Realistic and Romantic Schools

After we picked up the pearls from the snow, the secrets started to melt. There was no sun, but the white hills became a roaring river of brown slush. We stood on the bank and watched how, among empty bottles and pieces of wood, it carried away the dead angels who had been sleeping under the snow. How beautiful they are, we said, even in this dirty river, their broken wings remain white and their faces pristine. A few of us immediately went home so we could dream more angels, and we dreamed that we were lying at the bottom of an hourglass and that snow was falling from the bright opening in the sky above and covering us. Others rushed to get their fishing gear and started an angel hunting contest. They were joined by the butchers, who cut up the angels in front of photographers and enthusiastic crowds as soon as they were caught, separating pieces of meat from entrails and wings, which were auctioned later. These were the realists, people who loved angels up close and then burned them at the stake afterwards. We did no better either. The whiteness we died in was washed away, and suddenly we felt all the hooks that tied us, while we were still alive, to this one, therefore best world.

With Closed Eyes

When you close your eyes, you see a poem.
It has been emptied of the solidity of all the things you secretly want.
It reminds you of a newly painted white room
In which summer forgot to close the windows and door.
But this is just an inadequate allusion to images of the physical world.
There are no entrances or exits in this poem.
This poem only has substance in a gaseous state.
The people who float inside it, the metaphors
That hang on its walls could be
Instantly dispersed by a galactic wind and blend into something else.
Two naked clouds that have just started making love
Are scattered and blown by the stars into the cloud
Of a slaughtered pig surrounded by the grey cloud
Of the cigarette smoke of a father who observes everything,
Hidden in the dark corner of the poem. Most likely
He is the real author of every poem. You don't see him
In the darkness until he comes up
Silently from behind, playfully covers your eyes with his palms
And asks: Who am I? Will you kill me? Are you mine?

Thirst

When a black hour takes the colour of my blood on a red desk
When books don't open to speak but to whisper
When I become as wicked as
When every door closes and gasps in the darkness
When an orange is not an orange, a shoe not a shoe, and my shirt is put
    on in the morning by the one who will kill me in the evening
When I drink long gulps of water that fall into me like glass
When I am cut
When I don't believe in now, lose the before and don't see my reflection
    in shop windows
When someone starts to run after me, but just before he catches me I
    disappear again
When nothing whispers but everything is screaming because it is mute
When I am dicing an onion and think that the knife is the key with which
    I can open a wrist so that sand rushes from it
When Michelangelo touches Adam and goes through the world of cracks
When I am the left and right segments, the one that searches and the one
    that doesn't want to find
When I withdraw a finger and won't say *that's when* any more, no when,
    no bones, no one –
You

Lullaby

You have five minutes
Until I turn out the lights.
Because the poem you waited for all day
Isn't there, in the end simply list what *is*.
So: tired books on the table,
The plants have folded their leaves and gone to sleep,
The television rustles and a moth flutters over the table,
In love with light until death.
You have one minute. Thirty seconds.
Now I'm naked and in bed. I hear you:
Ten, nine, but – didn't I forget something? –
Six, yes, five, I forgot four,
Three, but now it's two and for this, too,
It's too late. I can just close my wings tight
And hope you wake me at zero.

Walnut

You've come away empty-handed and have a walnut in your hands.
At first you squeeze it and conceal it like some magic trick,
But then everything squeezes you and you know you must
Respond, and thus kill the magician, to survive.
In the centre of the walnut there's a kernel, but you don't care,
You need the solution written on the inside of the shell.
The distress is too much, so you squeeze the empty fist and break it.
The walnut goes silent, the broken signs become unfathomable
And the answer sphinx-like, but you slip inside through the cracks
And eat the kernel. Thus you carve out a space for yourself and become
      the kernel.
And the kernel becomes You. You crouches and waits
For the shell to heal around it. Like some foetus
It crouches and waits, and in the walnut there's less and less light
And fewer and fewer wounds. Slowly You can start to read the signs
And the signs are more and more whole.
You reads aloud, but when the ending almost arrives,
The shell heals and night falls around You. Caught in darkness, You hears
A white rabbit with murderous incisors hop out of a hat,
Stop in front of the walnut, and stare at it.

Kashmir

You appear there, where there are no letters, no numbers.
The light is too dark to see, or it is night.
There are no voices here. Sometimes someone sighs
And then a thousand mouths start to scream
Or to recite some anonymous poem.
There are no walls, no objects here, at least
You have not come across them. There is also no floor.
As if your body is constantly gliding through a swarm
Of fluttering butterfly wings or a cloud of rain.
Sometimes, when silence blows in with unknown names,
It seems to you that others must be here,
Similar to you, but you never meet anyone here,
Or you unwittingly pass through them, and it is at this moment
When you experience something like a thought or a dream or an emotion.
Sometimes you still had death and were afraid.
You thought that stuffed tigers' heads floated everywhere
And that each held one of your hearts between its fangs.
Now, amidst all the growling, you know what peace is.
Although you go and return, you are always here.
For here is not here. Here is
Kashmir.

A Thousand Doors

You awoke in a room with a thousand doors.
Behind every door is a long dark hallway.
You can choose any of them,
But when you open one of the doors and stare into the dark,
Someone tells you that if you enter, it won't be you
Who comes out on the other side. This happens to you
At every door and again and again you turn
And return and wait for another to decide.
Another arrives every night. Arrives and burns down
All thousand doors, one after the other, with dark fire.
All thousand doors burn down, but before your eyes
A thousand new, even more awful doors instantly grow.
So everything around you becomes larger and larger
And you curl into yourself until you don't close your eyes.
You will dream that the walls start to recede,
The ceilings grow through the stars, the floor vanishes into the soil.
You will dream and think that everything was only temporary,
Then you will open your eyes and think another's thoughts.

For You

Here, have a condom. You pretend you don't want it,
But in fact you need it. Take it. Like so.
Now read what's written on the silvery surface of the wrapper.
You don't understand the language, but you like it because you know
The words are meant for you.
Who knows, maybe they're even about you
Or were written with you in mind.
Open it. Without fake modesty. It's yours,
Do what you want with it. Like so.
Now put it to your mouth. No, no, you heard right,
Put it to your mouth. If you cannot do it this way,
Close your eyes and imagine
That you're holding a scrap of perfumed silk in your hands,
Or an ox-eye daisy that you want to kiss.
And now: blow. Yes, blow. Slowly. Wait until the breath
Carries everything you've gathered out of you. And so
It already grows. Blow even harder. See how big it's becoming?
Do you like it? That's enough now. It might expand
To fill the whole room, press you against the wall
And crush you. That's enough, I said. It's time
For you to tie it. Like soooo. Now it's truly
Yours, and you can do whatever you want with it.
Aaah, I see that you've taken red lipstick
And started to draw on it. You've drawn a dot.
And another. And underneath, a smile.
Now I understand. You'd like to draw me
And with that become my master, but you didn't quite
Get me right and now you're angry. You're furious.
But – what is this? It seems that behind my smile,
There, where there's nothing except your exhaled air,
There is something. You know this isn't possible, but still,
This feeling won't leave you. On the contrary:
You're increasingly overwhelmed and restless. You have the feeling
That you're lost in a dark forest
Or that you cannot move your limbs any more.

You hate yourself when you're like that, so you place your ear
To the mouth you drew for me, and listen intently.
The breath that you happily released earlier suddenly runs out.
Terrified, you listen again. Now
There is no longer any doubt. Someone is there
Inside the emptiness of the condom, and you damn well know
That where no one is, there can be only God.
Astonished, you move away, since you never expected,
Let alone predicted, something like that, and only now
Do you become truly furious. Even more: you are crazy with fear
Since you're not convinced that in a moment,
When you pull out a razor and cut slowly and deeply
Into me, I really will disappear forever.

Protuberances

(2002)

36 Seconds

I'm going to talk about the insects
That flew under a drunken sun, landed on us, drank our blood.
In the soft earth, sunk to our ankles,
You taught me how to set traps under heads of lettuce.
How to hold a knife. Cut an apple in two.
I got the first half,
You set the other, lethal one under a spring.
'So they won't eat what you grew,' you said,
Too naive and too good to see where and for whom you were setting it.
Hidden in my skull, it triggered years later and killed me
When I thought I finally loved and was loved.
In the first grade your sister taught me the names of flowers and shapes of
     letters,
Complex, incomprehensible ideas like *technology, history, God*.
That's when they built a slaughterhouse in our neighbourhood.
A record-breaking 36 seconds were needed
For a cow to be killed by a machine, strung up, skinned, and sawed into
     large pieces.
Mother, lately I don't know what's wrong with me.
I go to sleep early, and when I fall asleep, I walk, endlessly walk,
I don't know where, or to whom, but I persist, I walk and walk,
Until the buzzing of morning mosquitos wakes me and I know
That I must kill them, I must kill them all.

Zero Gravity

When I was a child
I read about the two ways that stars die.
In the first, the star begins to cool down.
Over millions of years it slowly loses heat and light.
All potential life dies out
Until it becomes infinite cold, the horizons of a dead giant.

In the other case, the star begins to contract.
Over millions of years, every atom, every speck of light,
Every wish, thought, hope compress into some non-existent centre.
The dying process ends when the entire star, together with its atmosphere,
Condenses to the size of a tennis ball.
Everything becomes one centre, infinite mass and gravity.

When I was a child
I read about both ways that stars die.
When the child disappeared, every birth became just an imitation
Of one of these two forms of death.
The emergence of civilisation. The origin of poetry.
I was born twice and my father twice gave up on me.
You stare at these books too much, he said, it's not good for your health.
It'd be better if you finally learned how to grip the racket properly
And hit the ball further than the net.

Citrus

On Saturday at three
In the supermarket.
You are still thinking about the chapter
On the creation of the universe.
You cannot envision the state
Before the Big Bang,
When the emerging cooling bodies
Were carried through space and time.
How to think *before* when before doesn't exist?
How, with words like *there* and *then*,
To step beyond? An image you don't see.

On Saturday afternoon, at three.
Among the shelves with pet food
And liquor bottles,
The fragility of bodies catches up with you.
Rarely astral,
Mainly chthonic.

On Saturday at three,
And only a metre away.
A stranger lies in a pool of blood.
The cashiers, who try to hold him
By his twitching limbs,
Have made a pillow with a bag of beans.
A wound has cut his face.
Red slime slowly covers your shoe.
You lift it. An imprint you don't understand.

In the supermarket.
On Saturday at three.
A bag with a kilogram of light is knocked over
And lemons explode like tiny suns
Around the shopping cart.
Thin peels of order

Quickly stop beside the cold cages of nonsense.
An event that evokes but doesn't explain.

At three. On Saturday.
In the car park it's raining.
It's January, too warm for this time of year.
On the television they wish
It were colder.
It would be good for winter tourism.
It would be good for the agricultural harvest.
It would be good for preventing viral illnesses.
On Saturday at three.

Protuberances

The silent explosions of ions. The suspension of energy in a sign.
Antigravity. Dance of magnetism in bone tumours.

Protuberances.

Visible to the naked eye only when the body is thrust into darkness,
When it is eclipsed and helpless, complete submission,
As when a patient submits to the indifferent hands of the nurses
Who close the door of the x-ray room behind them.
They leave him to himself and the machine,
Rubber fitted against his chest.
Radiation. Perhaps fatal.

Protuberances.

One hundred fifty million kilometres from the sun's chromosphere,
Masses of flammable gas rise for no real reason,
Etch a miraculous sign on the edge of the astral void,
Break off and fly into outer space at high speed.
Incandescence. Barely perceptible.

Protuberances.
Protuberances.

Be the word length of the light waves
That travel through memory and flesh,
Recording wounds to heal the names
Of the mutilations of this world.

Anticyclone

Meteorologists won't tell you
That snow has covered the forests.
But the fire in the stove remembers
I embraced the bark when the beeches still stood.

Chopped and sawed, stacked in piles –
It finally tried to pull me into the wound
That smouldered between its legs.
It sensed that I had agreed to the clear-cutting.

The hand follows the poker into the stove,
And the fire knows that the steel hook
Will leave no traces on its flames.
You and I: every touch forever recorded in the palm.

It took many years to finally burn you down.
Until today, when it snowed inside the house.

And no one, not even the gentlemen
Smiling sheepishly over their cyclone maps,
Knew how to say that in middle of the harshest winter
We continue touching with our burns.

Sandwerder

Last night the oaks in the yard awoke me.
Outside, in the treetops, I again heard
The rustling of my inner world.

It was a miraculous shift of perspectives,
As if I'd suddenly tightened a rusty lens.
What lay a long time indiscernible in the depth
Came to the surface. And became the surface.

In the morning I opened the door and sank
To my ankles in dark fallen leaves.
I parted them and stepped through two doors.
Through the first door into my world, which is,
And through the second same door into my world, which isn't.

Ptuj–Pragersko–Ljubljana

An unexpected cooling. A chain of Alpine peaks in the distance
And a hallucinogenic moon that hangs all day in the west.
You can feel it. Pressing like the solitary coin in your pocket.
The cashier pushed it towards you under the window,
Together with a ticket for the Ptuj–Pragersko–Ljubljana train.
The hole in the route tells you that somewhere a mistake has occurred.
Somewhere it's possible to return in time,
Erase yourself from the path you travelled,
Correct the route, begin again,
But you, left to the monotonous sadness of the rails, turned backward,
Quiet in the space and time you just left.
You lean your head against the rattling window, close your eyes.

In the middle of your forehead there's a resin mark
That a forester made with the swift blow of an axe on a crooked oak's trunk.
Lumberjacks are already coming through patches of snow and decaying leaves.
Squeezed into the knots of their bodies, with an unbearable longing for treetops
That makes their lips crack and sting.
They come when the trees are bare and asleep
And the bark doesn't sense their chainsaws' thirst.
The amputation occurs in frozen silence.
A child cuts his cake. The smell of gasoline goes quiet
And a giant's silent fall rustles through the air.

When the roots stir,
There will be only the faded marks of tractor tires
And a trunk's black trace in the undergrowth to recall
Whom they nourished so they could reach the sky through them.
Ptuj–Pragersko–Ljubljana.
Only one who departs among stumps knows the meaning of exile.
Everywhere unexpected coolings.
Chain marks on the stacked logs. Full moon.

Still Life

Words have no meaning.
They're keys to a place.

Though standing, you move.
Like the river moving beneath a pike's fin.

Her eye watches you from the ceramic sclera of a plate.
The locks grind bitterly between your teeth.

Plié

A hermetically sealed bottle.
Number 3 in the catalogue. Everything in its place.
When I lift it towards the light,
I can see your fingerprints on the glass from three winters ago.
Increasingly surrounded and covered by mine.
I remember you wanted to dance in the freezing air
When we bought it. You knew all along.

But regardless of the barking of young dogs and the changing weather,
The sprig of rosemary, preserved in burning liquid, stayed the same.
A dead stem that branches several times into an explosion of evergreen leaves,
An eternity of dead poets' verses that professors use to comfort the living.
I remember. Something in me turned.
Or I was already constantly turning
And only then saw the end of the pedicle,
Which had detached from the concave bottom.
The leaves started to slide slowly over the memory of our hands
And stopped when it became too narrow.

When I started to name myself,
The words did not want to pass through my throat.
There is no room
For pirouettes in the drop of air
Beneath the merciless cork.

Between Bread and Salt

I see you.
In the kitchen, as if standing inside a giant teardrop,
You peel off dead skin, set the onions flat on the wood,
Slice them, chop them, and lower them ethereally into the oil.

Outside, the rain has stopped drumming, like that night in Trujillo.
A torrent carried half the coastal graveyard away.
When the waters receded, coffins stuck out of the mud like broken trunks.
The dead could finally gaze straight at the sky in peace.

Whatever effort I made to bend my joints,
Strain my muscles, set off, leap out of myself:
The earth held me more firmly than I did,
Wrapped in a red cashmere scarf,
Holding a kitchen knife with the inscription *Made in Vienna*.

I see you.
You just wiped its broad blade on your white apron.
Put it down on the table. Turned away.

Whatever happens:
In the whole world there isn't a knife that shouldn't be put down some day.
And the world is an onion.
Full of regret, you cut into its frail, uneven spheres
And peel it off between bread and salt.

Your full mouth peels reality:
Swallow your words to the end and keep your hands empty,
Stand in the clear distance, stand and stand,
And repeat the name of a centre that does not exist,
Repeat the name of the emptiness
That remains. And nothing more.

Returning Home

On the winding metal staircase
Rust blossoms around
Pots of wilted flowers.

Suitcases full of dirty laundry
And old questions make me stagger.
As if I were moving unease from threshold to threshold.

We were quiet the last four hundred kilometres.
Neither of us knows if we can conceal
Even the silence of arrival.

The face in the bathroom mirror
That I ran so far away from
Did not lose sight of me even for a moment.

Europe

You're still peddling the story that the Turks
Knocking down their tents at the gates of Vienna was just a trick.
That they are disguised as kebab vendors
Still on the hunt for the right moment
To rush from their kiosks and cut your senile neck.

Although your tribes got lost forever
In the marshes of your barbaric intentions
And you yourself cannot tell the skull of a Goth
From the skull of a Slav from the skull of an Anglo from the skull of a Frank,
You still believe you're restored only by the death of your sons.

You still think you will fool us all.
When I close my tired eyes, you appear
In the image of a large, obscene woman who gives birth while snoring
And a man who secretly masturbates in the dark beside her,
Thinking of America.

The Book of Things

(2005)

A

A died. And didn't die. Like his father
A, like his grandfather he drowned in the village graveyard.

Drowned but didn't drown. He went into the mud.
Into the mud and into the dumb stones in the mud.

Silent there now. Forgetting. Erasing. Is there now and isn't.
Because there is no place. He is without beginning and end. A-A-A.

Someone died. No one. His name – forgotten.
Like his father's and his grandfather's name. Sometimes

A a rattling of things. The one who went to bed
Sometimes gets up, the one who keeps vigil continues dying.

Sometimes A-A-A the unbearable terror of space searching for its voice.
Sometimes A-A-A the monotonous sadness of rain over streets.

A-A-A gurgles when it rolls out of the sea.
A-A-A the sigh of quartz in watches.

Surely it is only – A is dead.

Whoever thinks he sometimes hears him should listen with the other ear,
Whoever doesn't hear him will go on listening in vain.

Egg

When you kill it at the edge of the pan, you don't notice
That the egg grows an eye in death.

It is so small, it does not satisfy
Even the most modest morning appetite.

But it already watches, already stares at your world.
What are its horizons, whose glassy-eyed perspectives?

Does it see time, which moves carelessly through space?
Eyeballs, eyeballs, cracked shells, chaos or order?

Big questions for such a little eye at such an early hour.
And you – do you really want an answer?

When you sit down, eye to eye, behind a table,
You blind it soon enough with a crust of bread.

Knots

There are knots whose artistry you know by heart.
And another kind that come from Smyrna.

There are sisters you won't free from your memory.
And brothers, bound to you back to back.

And mothers, woven into tattered sweaters.
And fathers, tossing at night in their own traps.

For these knots are like someone
Secretly led a rope through your ear.

As if you were this rope and the knots your family.
They are not of Gordian origin and do not come from Smyrna.

They are from near and far, and easily and with effort
They settled in you. A short time ago, since forever.

Be patient with your knots.
Let them grow, let them tighten in peace.

The day comes when the rope rises up in drowsy silence.
Like a fakir you climb out of your self.

Stone

No one hears what the stone keeps to himself.
Insignificant, it is only his, like pain,
Caught between the leather of a shoe and the sole.

When you slip it off, leaves spin in bare alleys.
What was, will never be again,
And piles of others are signs in decay.
The smell of nearby clinics. Mute, you go on.

What you keep to yourself, no one hears.
You are the only inhabitant of your stone.
You just threw it away.

Grater

You remember how your mother, Jocasta,
Returned from the pigsty with a gaping palm.

Inside the madness of pain a window opened.
She stepped out and stepped out of her body.

You remember how your startled father was changing a bandage,
How, mid-escape, the edges of the bandage turned red.

This time the grater's whisper is yours. The world is being whittled away.
The apple wedge is getting smaller, but who is there for whom?

Are you merely an instrument of the apple in your palm?
Silently it grates you, a ripe buddhist, idared samsara.

When it vanishes you, you open your eyes, like your mother
That time, on the other side of the wound.

Urinal

The backs of male shadows amidst the stink of urine.
Like some firing squad, staring
At the multiplying ceramic tiles.

The wall stretches out in front of you, too.
A fish is pushing her white head through
From the other side, doesn't penetrate.

She wants to drink up the whole world, which she carries,
To release the surplus human weight.
Who knows, perhaps she already did so long ago.

And aren't the faces of the men urinating
Reflections of Jonah's, squeezed between fishy spikes?
What is here, what there?

What kind of human voice is on the other side of the urinal?
Are people happier, more timeless there, fish Fa?
Or there is no other side,

And they are only the visions of drunks, tensed in fear
That you don't close your thirsty mouth, Faronika,
As fair punishment for grinding your yellowed teeth,

And castrate us.

Chocolate

He died in order to be the bar of chocolate in front of you.
He wishes that you too would consume the anguish of his death.

Limitlessly. That fear and deliverance would melt in your mouth.
His sweet entrails, the bitter curves of his concoctions.

He asks you to unwrap him, to reveal yourself in the proper light.
Beyond kindness. Beyond mercy and forgiveness.

The two of you touch wordlessly, in the tongue of mute gifts.
What you break and eat, breaks and feeds on you.

Your saliva, the secret feeling of an empty mouth is his.
Your fingers, which search for him in drawers. But not the reverse.

You must remain hungry so that god can still give.
And what your god once gave, he endlessly takes.

Raisins

Whose veins, whose loves, whose traces,
Whose time evaporated in the wrinkles of raisins.

The cool grains of past summers. You eat them and you eat.
As you would eat the fingertips of god, who holds all.

Reduced to the utter humility of the aged.
Like handfuls of pensioners on a pilgrimage.

They rise from the table and plunge into your roof.
The whole bunch rises. Truly rises.

Whose arteries, whose fears, whose traces,
Whose gargling you gulp down with the wrinkles of raisins.

The aged fingers grab you from within,
Choking you until you spit out their name.

Ant

It clings to objects tenaciously.
They shift about slowly, it moves with them,
Like the invisible moving through the visible world.

Hair for a blade. A beetle's body for wheat grain. Trace for trace.
So it rises, what you call home.
The border between the safety of tunnels and the unbearable expanse.

It returns from far away, always by the same way.
And it brings no messages. And no prophecies.
A period at the end of an increasingly intricate clause.

And there aren't names for what it is.
When it disappears into its maze, only hope remains
That at least there are names for what it isn't.

Umbrella

In the afternoon he rises from the silence in the corner.
Smiling mercifully like Saint Sebastian.

When he takes your palm, the world turns on itself.
Outside he unbuttons his too-tight tuxedo.

You step inside him as into a childhood lair.
You duck among the arrows that pierce his ribcage.

The sheltering shadow swallows up rain clouds.
As if stones would drip from the ground, drizzle on his skin.

The arrows groan if they touch the brow of the one walking among them.
Then the pain is sweet. Then it is sexy to be a martyr.

He suffers gladly, so that you don't have to fall into the sky.
He indulges in your pressure when cars drive past.

You stop and listen to the blunt booms between his ribs.
Beating like the ventricles of two hundred pedophiles before an infarct.

Although it is cool. Cool and tight.
And there is no heart. No internal organs.

As if amidst nothing nothing extends to the body.
As if knives would slide inside the surface of the wind.

Sometimes he borrows your mouth for his own quackish voice.
You open them like fish then, but it is not prayer that comes out.

Gargling. Stuttering. Mumbling.
As if someone were drowning in your head in his chest in your palm.

Finally he bursts out laughing.
At which, at whose end?

The sky watches you blackly from puddles.
You will go there, from where heaven climbs wetly along your trouser leg.

Bread

Every time, he leads you into temptation to become a gentleman
Who feeds on crumbs under his servant's table.

He asks you to do him harm, for you to stab him,
To shred him to pieces, consume his still warm body.

Without shame he appears to you naked as at Creation.
He is a pervert. He provokes you with abstinence.

But he is being given you and you give. And every morning
And every evening you repeat the floury game.

He made you into a crematory of guilt.
When he feeds you, you speak and instantly are more famished.

Yes, yes, he loves you, that is why he accepts your knife.
He knows that all his wounds crumble in your hands.

Hand Dryer

Who speaks when you are not speaking in your own name?
When you do not pretend to speak in the name of another,
But there is the presence of a voice like the ghost's at a séance?
Just *retro larifari, cadabra abra, aha, aha, blah blah*?

It happens, as if the wind would speak through you.
As if the bora speaks, the Košava, the Passat, icy Siberian winds.
It happens, invisible while speaking in a clear voice.
And they do not happen. Their returns bring no changes.

Or indeed, somewhere between, where the living brush against the dead.
Drops, with which you have sprinkled their brow, evaporate from your palms.
Again you press the silver button on the plastic box.
Again they come roaring, this time to warm your frigid fingers.

Just *abracadabra, aha, aha, blah blah*. Because they bring nothing new.
The petrol station toilet is just like before.
And you, too, were not changed. Only through your palms did something
    blow.
You do not hold him, but sometimes he holds you. He has your life lines.
    Your handshake.

He has no name, he who speaks when you do not speak in your name.
And no home. And no things of his own.
A no-name without a body, always on the road.
And his paths can also be yours, but yours can never be his.

Stomach

What does the clerk of the stomach say?
That yesterday he was seen crossing the street.
That he didn't pay the toothpick at the restaurant.
That he is flying too high and it will happen to him sooner or later.

What do the veal steak and two flasks of Teran say?
That the light suddenly ran out.
That it grew tight and stuffy, though you still didn't leave.
That it is sad when you drop so low.

What does the thigh, which grazes behind the cow's head, say?
That his gross worth grows with every morsel.
That he will enter the souls of fifteen wedding guests and two dogs
    simultaneously.
That it isn't cold as long as there's enough grass and roads on the horizon.

And what does this gurgle, this drooling stutter whisper to you?
That it isn't cold as long as there's enough meat and potatoes.
That it is sad when you drop so low.
That all creatures which fly sooner or later will fall.

Pupa

The growing presence of the butterfly in her
Does not fill her with fear.
She hangs in her cocoon world like some religious fanatic,
And this world inside another, larger cocoon.
Through this cocoon you walk home.

Your step seems firmly pressed into time,
But in truth you recognise only the pins
With which small tortoiseshell, admiral, peacock
Are impaled on the wall.
Your ignorance only grows.

How many cocoons enclose the last one?
When do seconds die?
In whose sleep do clouds arise?
Isn't it insignificant, the likelihood
That one day we will fly away?

Knives

They hang there freshly sharpened.
In the glimmering light. Light.

The butcher's shop is a big family enterprise.
Two million butchers and customers.

Customers and butchers. You hardly discern them.
For some are others. And others are others.

The buyer puts on the blood-stained apron.
The butcher opens a purse for a still-twitching shoulder.

The knives watch you coldly, with closed eyes.
They remember where they were, what they mediated.

If you grab them, you feel a slight shiver in the handles.
At dusk the blades reflect the deaths into which they were thrust.

But where are the bones? Where are the names?
Look, look, they are also stuck in your throat.

And when you speak, you also speak with the silence of the murdered.
They are stuck in your duodenum.

And when you need to go, you shit what was slaughtered before your birth.
They are scattered in your shallow chest.

And when you get off in haste after urgent business,
It is not cans and brushwood that crack under your feet.

Where are they? Where are they? Where are they?
Everyone knows about them. No one remembers.

Jelly

Some were on their way through Tivoli,
In the middle of gymnastics on rings,
In the middle of lion taming at the circus
When bones leaped out of their shoulders.

Others got greasy fingers while making deals.
Small bones spurted from their palms.
Knuckles were bent by the pressure
Like sealing wax.

Left under desks and altars, vertebrae pooled.
Astonished heads collapsed into themselves
Like wet paper sacks.
Teeth dangled in the middle of a sentence.

Dialects evaporated discreetly.
Then amoebae, bacteria and algae began to multiply
Until jelly flooded the streets.
Whoever touched someone stuck to him forever.

Bandage

Every morning she covers your head. And presses, presses.
Owing no one, you must pay everyone.

But not like the wounded one at the front. No one turns his head after you.
And not like someone who smacks against the door-jambs of confessionals.

Silently and slowly the sky collapsed on you,
So that you alone do not know, why your bandage.

You grope for her. You search. You try to take her off, you tear,
Because you do not know if she is hiding a wound, if she hides anything.

Your fingers stretch into the void, become tangled, like politicians.
Your thoughts just accumulate new knots in the head.

Like women who go home with jugs on their heads,
You wander the globe with your bandage.

But the fountains dried out long ago.
Without borders you have nowhere to go.

Mint

Mintafiction, minthane, mintabolism.
There the smell of mint grows out of bone,
Out of a neighbour's thumb and a stranger's shin.
No animal could do it, it's not worth repeating.

Mintatax, mintasound, mintaphysics.
For what stays, when only plants try
To heal a musician's rib and the mayor's skull.
No laxative could do it, it's not worth mentioning.

Even less who will remember, cannot forget
Endless fields of mint, ruts, indifference.
Mintamen. Mintanight. Mintanaught.
No dictionary could do it, it's not worth noting.

Shoes

They protect you
So that the road presses softly on you.
Messengers that swish between you
And the world of trails that erase each other.
Made out of skin and sutures.
And yours are stitched from the words *skin and sutures.*
Protect them.
You can be naked and without anything,
But with shoes on your feet you will never be poor,
Never remain hidden,
Knocked down under a bed,
Abandoned in an armoire, forgotten in an attic.
Sleep with them.
Bathe in the shoes,
Make love with them on.
Let them always warn you
That you are only here on a brief visit.
Soon you will have to walk on.
Never take them off.
When you take them off, the journey will have ended.
They bury you like a gypsy,
Barefoot and without a name.

Sea Horse

Creatures of liquid light, vagabonds of underwater currents,
Students of belly dancing, the ocean's brides loyal to his moods.

With their final breath, forgotten Phoenician gods
Inflated glassy bodies that shine like empty clepsydrae.

Tails wrap playfully around the mesh in fishing nets,
The tiny wings' fluttering sketches pillows of eternity in the restless sleep
    of the drowned.

They are princes of confidence. And when the female spawns eggs into
    the male
So that he bears them and gives birth, they are the social democratic ideal
    of reproduction.

Too fragile for guilt, but noticeable enough
That the jealous eye of the blue mussel thinks of beauty and love.

Among the shadows of people, sea horse bodies dry,
Lose translucence, become rough and blunt.

Between two fingers you crush them, beauty and love,
Into what is not beautiful and what (you don't remember when) stopped
    loving.

Saliva

Not just birth, and copulation and death.
Birth, copulation death.

There is also spitting. After all, everywhere, always.
The marking of death and stirring the dead.

Lazarus rise. Lazarus sit down. Lazarus rise. Lazarus sit down.
It regenerates in your mouth.

It pours, this poisonous, sweet force.
Between teeth, when you spit your own little genocide.

You push it with the tongue. Pour resin over it, phlegm of words.
Him, who raises into birth. Into copulation.

And him, who sits down into *s*. Who sits down.
Who slips to an unknown place, so that you swallow deeply.

You hiss, for you know each other inside out.
He lurks in the mirror. Waits to spit in your face.

Toothpick

A bit of undigested meat has got lost
And is calling for a revolt.

Rebellious foreign body. It signals from your mouth.
Although you do not speak.

Although you allowed no one to speak
In your name.

But it keeps yelling,
Incites an uprising, applies pressure.

You try to remove it with the tongue,
But there are no words that would silence its protest.

A little Robespierre in Polyphemus' mouth.
But without sly fortune, without gods and flocks on his side.

You extract him from your conscience, grind what is gnawing you.
Down with the revolution.

Although the last linden falls.
You sprawl on her stump, break off a splinter and belch.

The toothpick juts from your mouth like a centurion's spear,
Which cleansed the empire.

The black hole in the tooth whispers:
This kingdom also will collapse on itself one day.

Cork

He was extracted from a tree, ground and made anew
To protect access to mystery like the last seraph.

You never know which side he's on.
On the side of memory, on the side of oblivion.

He guards the world from the genie of Aladdin's lamp,
Closes firmly so that Pandora's evil spirits don't flee.

Or is evil already on this side from the beginning
And does the cork protect the last refuge of silence?

Anyhow. The fat innkeeper's fingers drilled him, pulled,
And pushed again with the bloody side turned to you.

What was stored in safety escaped.
It swooshed down the throat like emptiness into the bottle.

The cork in her mouth still bleeds.
And still silent, you swallow.

The voices of fugitives from neighbouring tables grow distant,
The consolation of the bottle, that the message in her didn't travel in vain.

Windscreen Wipers

Both of them hide something,
That is why they move in such harmony.
Like two serfs in black rubber boots.
They get up to go immediately back to bed.

Bits of mud. Drops. Drops. Insects smeared.
They wipe but cannot erase.
Because there is no one who could grant them the power of absolution.
Their goal of clear vision is complete delusion.

No one frees himself following the world's flashes.
They slip over the windshield to an unknown place.
Your guilt is transparent. Watertight. Inspected.
When it bursts into dust you forget you exist.

Hayrack

Guardian of the land.
Guardian of the land's inhabitants.
Guardian of their consciences.
When everyone sleeps, the hayrack pays attention
So that no one slips away from the game,
Misses the return of King Matjaž.

Slovenian heroes sacrificed their lives
So their sons could freely dry
The contents of their skulls
In the Alpine breeze of the hayrack's rungs.
The vast meadows are their souls.
Cows chew and shit them
And out of cow shit their souls grow
Still more beautiful and succulent.

Oh, hayrack, *yes*, hayrack.

No one knows who was the first to build bridges,
Who knitted the first walkways,
Raised the first carrier pigeon,
Invented the doorknob and opened a neighbour's door.
But only a Slovene could construct
A prison in the middle of open country,
A cage that divides the world:
On one side hypocrisy,
On the other a chronically inflamed prostate.

Hayrack. Hayyyyrack. Hay-raaaa-ck.

Your mother, insanity,
Squeezes you to herself when you are sad and yearn.
She lets you eat edges and drink morphield.
Because it is nothing. Don't be afraid. Don't cry, she tells you.

The enemy is constantly everywhere,
But he cannot get to you as long as
Brigadiere Hayrackino, Hauptmann Hayracker,
Ezredes Häyräckek and Pukovnik Hayrakić protect you.

You sigh.

In the distance, mountains.
In overcoats, moths.
In the poem, gold.

You sneeze.

You scratch under your navel and know:
Together you will make it.

Wheelbarrow

It lies tipped over at the edge of a slope.
The wheel turns, blinded in the wind.

A mouth vomited like after chemotherapy.
Now already whispering again, but without relief.

It isn't a Homeric hero. It has the stomach of a clumsy ram
That smuggled something larger and heavier than itself.

All to this point, where their trace goes silent
And it must outwit the gaze, outwit the word.

Cargo begins to gather back uphill.
The wounds heal, as if they are only on paper.

Earring

The whole time he tells you what to do.
His voice is chocolate candy filled with hysteria.

He is a loving blackmailer. An owl blind in one eye.
It is enough that he sees half the world to command the other half.

He gladly inspects himself in the mirror, but goes crazy if you praise him
Before another. He is not your property. He is not your adornment.

He coos only when you dance and when you make love with him.
Then cages open. Then he is the white message bearer of the gods.

Gradually you detach him more often, hide him in a box, misplace him.
But his bite at the lobe still whispers to you.

As if Eros holds you with invisible filigree pliers
And solders words of guilt and the silence of betrayal into your ear.

A copy of a stone from Sisyphus' mountain is set inside it.
You roll hope uphill. And you roll downhill drunk, despondent and alone.

Salmon

After years of living in the ocean
Pacific salmon swim up the river
Whose current brought them down.

It takes weeks, their journey to the source,
To the place where the first eye shadowed
In featureless roe.

They do not gather more food.
They do not follow everyday survival strategies.
They do not search, do not flee, do not hunt. They are on the way.

Gradually their skin goes blood red.
Their heads turn green.
The male's mouth grows hooked and long.

Visible to all, they travel.
By jumping up waterfalls
They wound themselves to death by the thousand.

The rest swim further through rapids,
Towards the brown wavy hair, the shadow that awaits them,
Bent over the arch of their rushing world.

How delicate is the death of wild red salmon
Impaled on bears' claws.
As if death is not the end, but a mute passage.

And Destrnik is a place in the heart of Alaska.

The cub stands on the bank
And watches his mother, who has bewitched the river.
Her offspring already on his own.

Rapids, waterfalls, the deadly blows of paws.
Salmon seldom manage to return to their source,
Conclude beginning and end under their fins.

By spawning they die off slowly in icy waters.
Bloated, they spread in pools.
You walk against the current, which takes them. Which takes you.

Shit

Children happily rummage through him for a sign.
Provence's princesses made compresses
Of eternal youth with him.
In the spring he is scattered on fields and corn grows.

At a sharp pain you look back happy.
But it is not shit that you see, that looks at you.
Your muddy soul climbed out of you.
Your only true child. He fell from you.

Without a soul you are form without value.
That is why you lose it and create. Lose and create.
You do not exchange your shit for gold.
You exchange your shit only for love.

Paper Clip

You put down the paper confused.
You only now notice the rusty imprint of a paper clip.
A spiral sign for the way inward.

She held together scraps of the world like an invisible thread.
She warmed you, so enveloped in herself. Like a foetus.
Like a snail. Like a body in a mass grave.

Her intention is not to add or take away from the world.
Not a creator, the little paper clip. She only causes contact.
Someone removed her. Who, why – you don't know.

Nor how many sheets were lost.
With a finger you go over the trace and start to read again.
Before you opens a space within a space within a space.

This poem has no end.

Aspirin

It's enough. Otherwise no, you didn't expect
That it would end now, in such a way, but it's enough.

You will dissolve between thoughts watching you more inanely,
Between words, which concealed no one's silence.

This is nothing fatal. Your departure will be quiet and inconspicuous.
No rooster will take off, no one will sneeze behind you.

It will just rustle in some corner, as if water were poured on aspirin.
A white coin from Noah's ark tossing in a glass.

Her passengers and messages won't last.
Particles of the pill will dissolve like cypress wood.

The secret of life is not to remain the same. The same. The same.
The secret of life is that you rustle. Shhhh.

Enough. It's enough. Drink from your poverty. Until empty.
You won't escape with hemlock or some other ruse.

No one ferries you. No one will be saved.
Only thirst will be appeased. At least for the moment.

Parcel

It travelled from afar only to test you.
Two by three by six centimetres, with no addressee.

Why did your name wrap itself in silence
As if abducted in a parcel, mouth taped?

Two gazes by three solitudes is six obsessions.
Six chances divided by day and night – roughly infinite.

But perhaps No One's name is in the parcel
And yours is the inner side of the fold, which envelops it?

If you observe it from outside, you can guess, but you do not know.
If you open it, you can stammer ragged vocals, but you do not compose.

Chair

The rings in it make time look aside.
It recalls you, when you were still a primate. On all fours.
And current sapiens.
Drunk, tormented, desperate. On all fours.
A human with the perspective of floors. Of you.

It wears anal histories.
The leather skirt of a Roman centurion has warmed it.
And a few scraps on the naked buttocks of a serf.
The stiff flaxen pants of SS Senior Storm Leader
And the prancing edge of sticky miniskirts.

It knows as many stories as backsides.
But even the fronts got lost. Drifted away in rough waters.
So be grateful that it has accepted you as you are.
That it bears you. Now, when at last all is behind you,
You can entrust it with your weight, lean a head,

Slightly confused from the noises of centuries. Snore.

Candle

When someone dies, it is not day not night.
And no one present. Not here not there.
A small flicker above the gas stove.

Unimportant. And it does not live and did not die,
What you conceal with a palm.
It does not ask, does not give answers.

It is not on the side of good. It is not on the side of evil.
It does not know lies. Not truth, not sense or nonsense.
It is not the future and not the past.

It is and at the same time is not. Not that it is or wouldn't be you.
It will not be by itself or something else.
Not air not fire. Not light not flame.

Not abyss not hope. Not yes not no.
When someone dies, someone has not died yet.
He climbed down the wick inside himself.

You reach behind and extinguish him.

The Book of Bodies

(2010)

The children in our village

The children in our village feared a man who never spoke. Hunched, he would just grin silently now and then. Many times, someone furtively threw a stone at him, and we crossed to the other side of the road as he slowly hobbled towards us. He died as he had lived, quiet and lonesome, and to this day he remains the village's only resident whose name I never learned.

The two-headed wolf in *The Kunstkamera* of Peter the Great, Ritta and Christina Parodi in the Parisian *Muséum National d'Histoire Naturelle*, pairs of foetuses in formaldehyde in the Berlin *Museum of Medical History at the Charité*. Teratology cannot explain if two creatures grew together or if they were one that never split all the way. What does the Creator's plan have in store for them? The unborn who for centuries haven't been able to die. It's not death, but birth, that's mysterious.

Years ago I went to the maze of mirrors in the Viennese *Prater*. A reflection of me as a blimp in one mirror stretched to touch the ceiling in another, and in a third, and in the reflection my head inflated, making us laugh. Searching for the exit, I leaned against one of the mirrors. Our bodies grew together. Perhaps they were never separated before and the mirrors were there only to conceal the dimension of time.

The road leads past the English row house we once lived in. In a year and a half, I didn't see anyone enter or exit the house next door. But sometimes, on clear mornings, or after a rain, a man's cry broke from behind a thin wall, so desperate it chilled me to the bone.

Nails are the biggest mystery. I trim them over and over, but they stubbornly escape from my skin. As if they feared the body. They suggest that I also fear it, suspicious of those whom mute organs hide. Later I read that in Denmark in 1995, during the autopsy of a boy's brain, the remains of 21 foetuses were found. His unborn brothers and sisters. The mystery is birth.

For two days I've been cleaning

For two days I've been cleaning the house the tenants left. In a back room, under the radiator, I find a one-cent coin and two paperclips stuck together, a couple embracing endlessly. I wring the cloth after cleaning the floor, black water and sand flow down the bathtub drain. All I do is move dust.

I'm watching *Lost Highway* when the phone rings. The voice says Svetlana died on her way home the other night. The voice knew her for thirty-five years. There's much guilt for what was said to her during their last conversation, that she ate too much and was an insufferable nag.

When someone dies, this is our first thought: where did I last see this person, what did we talk about? A place which gets its own 'last time'.

At the end we expect the words of a prophet, a theatrical farewell and a grand closing act. But someone falls asleep just as they fell asleep night after night for six, seven decades. Someone else is driving down a highway, his heart fails, the car hits the guardrail. It's not clear if the impact entered the consciousness of the dead.

What did I tell him the last time we met? Did I overlook something, an ambiguous clue, a message for the survivors? Shouldn't I always, in every conversation, utter words with a consciousness of finality? What would that change? Wouldn't the incessant threat of the last word be exactly what introduces theatricality into a conversation, makes communication impossible? Doesn't speaking mean speaking unfinished matters? And shouldn't I first ask what the end really is, if it's all just moving dust?

Your private apocalypse

Your private apocalypse amid blooming daffodils. In a book, airline coupons. In a pocket, foreign currencies. In you, a dark tunnel you call memory. Snow on this day last year, you say. We live in the chaos of the sun. To leave means to turn a new page. On Sunday, at East Coker. But there, as if arched past the last horizon, instead of the sermon on unconditional love, the ocean murmurs. Another attempt to languish in calyces, the night unfurls.

It's necessary to add only fourteen hidden stations between St Albans and salvation. No distance between them, only the word *jurnée*. I could, if I weren't there, if 'there' weren't ever more distant, and if the likelihood that space doesn't exist didn't course through me by faith in the letter, I could, if were I again on the forgotten, missed path, if 'there' were 'here', in this cell, this letter, where the parchment ends. Over its margins crashes my life, named William Paris. There, here, a sewn pleat at the end of an undersized *mappa mundi*. The territory of an angel's feather, the death of the rectangle.

On Good Friday we go to Sainsbury's. Then we eat the thick silence of vacuum-packed chicken guts. On a walk, you want memories from particular perspectives. I withdraw into cynicism, but eventually give in, lean my head against damp English soil. In a dorm room, we awkwardly tear off each other's clothes. Your nails dig into my thigh, I hug you and we exchange saliva like two calves.

An article about identical twins. The elder is obsessed with drawing self-portraits on ostrich Easter eggs. The younger writes the word *nails* into the fire during a voodoo ritual, and Jesus is instantly nailed. Frightened and marked with guilt, the younger brother Christ takes off into the sky. The first cosmonaut, soon to be followed by his loyal dog Laika.

I deny it, because it doesn't help, though it flares up again and again, this feeling that there, where my body ends in your body, there's no end. And it's not religion, it's only a tiny, sweet consolation when you fall asleep in my arms, that there will always be this wind rustling through the slender bodies of the young birches of Grantchester, the bent buttercup blossoms in April dew, cumuli, cumuli and you, smiling in some forgotten, already faded photograph.

For whom do the angels play?

For whom do the angels play? They are so skeptical of the self-aggrandisement of saints, immersed in their wrongs and punishments, in their paths to God, the supreme autoeroticist and exhibitionist. Only Job, the patron saint of quivering lute strings and violin-plucking, who suffered so successfully that now he can protect music and the muses, comes close to Him. Almost as naked as Bellini's Signor in the Accademia in Venice.

No difference between voice and body. Thus Hayden plays his saxophone in the Hotel Europa Regina. Strangeness spills from his mouth down the golden curves of the instrument, from afar it bites through skin and organs, appearing from the bones. It appears without puncturing anything, transforms the air into ecstasy, the reed, the voice, as if repositioning itself, pledging itself. Keys. Reed. Eyelids. Voice. Keys. Mouth. Voice.

The streets are so narrow that two people meeting at the same time must exhale to slip by. Only the smell and the voice keep it all in check. Exhausted from wandering, we come for the third time to the same campanile. A curving with no way out. Without shaking the mortar, a woman's voice penetrates the brick wall. A lonely melody. Then a brief plucking of strings and the awakening of no one.

The frequency by which the universe oscillates. Now caught by the contrabass. If I turned up the amplifier's volume a little, the membranes of the speakers would burst like the membrane of my right middle ear when I dove. The voices were calling me deeper. And there, at the bottom, lay a black box, perhaps an old transistor, a black hole that transmitted nothing, a passage where every melody, even angelic ones, disappears.

The most horrifying moment, when I was three years old and first heard a recording of my own voice. I covered my ears and threw myself screaming to the ground. I was dissected like some thing, turned inside-out to the world. And the whole world, strangely dead, slipped into me. Neither wailing nor covering my ears could prevent the violence of this act. I still hear its echo in me. Keys. Mouth. Voice.

I wake up without my right hand

I wake up without my right hand. A strange hand beneath my head. It just dangles when my left hand lifts it. Two hands, I have the living one, the dead one has me. Then blood pumps the end through the veins, spills it through the body. The boundary of belonging blurs, but only briefly. As if the circulatory system were an ancient, undeciphered language. Who guards its code? The hand slowly squeezes me, finger by finger, into a fist.

The right angel amid hundreds of marks, the only figure among letters. First, the salesman stamps wings twice on the article about the right to unannounced military intervention in crisis zones, then a third time on his palm. When I pay, he wraps the stamp in used newspaper, but how am I to take the angel from his palm? The pale blue indigo of the angel's trumpet on the stamp announces the edge of my presence here. Everything that has ever taken possession of me has been tossed over this edge, into a chasm. My life is waiting for a shining midday, when the bones strike the bottom and I burst like the letters of an unknown alphabet.

Our bodies are only vague metaphors of some initial fissure. But the first division must happen somewhere. If I could see without vision, perceive without senses, move beyond flesh beneath transparent skin, think without meaning – would I transcend the lapse of the mysterious bond between a language that designates and a name that never speaks? From somewhere a shadow creeps into this poem. No one cast it. But from where and for what this firing squad, an instantaneous silence and a shot, even though it says nothing?

The left angel. I caught sight of it only after a month of sleeping beneath its face. In the studio, the architect had kept part of the old beams of the monastery, where executions had taken place during the revolution. The spirits of the dead keep walking the corridors. I wake up, but not completely. I look around the ruins of my dreams, from which I was taken. One of the spirits guides me to a pair of leaf-coloured stains on an old beam, the shadow of an angel with a trumpet. The fissures announce time as recognition of what is shrouded. Time, which will have to occur again and again, the absent participle of the future perfect tense.

In the fifth week of pregnancy, an embryo measures a good four millimetres. The placenta looks like a tiny bubble. In it, the shadow of a grain. I try to visualise cell division, growth and the stages at which organs, eyes, both arms, fingers develop from the gametes. In the fifth week, all this is only bare possibility, a plan inscribed into an embryo. A bare, still unmarked temporality. But a heart has already formed, already beats. Here, imagination ends. What command selects a pair of cells to begin a regular beat? What possibilities are concealed by the particles, which my language calls negligible? Isn't every diacritical mark, every dust particle, every fleeting thought potentially the heart of an embryo? And what does this mean for the poem, the bearer of messages?

Many weeks nothing

Many weeks nothing, then, like an eye, the beginning of a poem spots me on page 1710 of the journal *Philosophical Transactions: Biopolitical Sciences*: 'Anatomically speaking, modern man originated approximately 200,000 years ago, when he was already some six million years separated from his ancestors, common to both humans and chimpanzees. The reason for the evolutionary advantage of modern man is unknown. The latest hypothesis revolves around the so-called "language gene" FOXP2, the mutation of which produced various language and speech limitations. The gene contains a protein with 715 amino acids and is similar to other relatives of regulatory genes, which are involved in the development of the embryo. The human version of FOXP2 has probably existed less than 200,000 years, implying its involvement in the process of natural selection, the product of which is modern man.'

At first I thought it was the sound of birds, but then it dawned on me that it was the shouts of the undocumented immigrants who for weeks had been sleeping in the park beneath my window. Were they only arguing about where to sleep before the treetops were bent and the hailstorm unleashed its grey lattice across the city? Beneath the stomping storm their voices grew only more furiously desperate, they under the trees in the downpour, my academic neighbours and I behind windows. At the first drops the windows were quietly closed and the building turned into an illuminated gallery of baroque portraits of merchants and city gentlemen, debt collectors, tax collectors, and inquisitors, until out of shame the lights were switched off, one by one, before the eyes of those who had nothing.

Perhaps I am only dreaming about the traffic accident. I cannot wake up, cannot move my limbs, my lips remain immobile, my eyelids too. I hear and see everything, the paramedics, the respirator pulled over my face, the bright blue walls of the intensive care unit, the visits and crying of my family. And so in sleep many years pass. Fewer and fewer visitors. I still cannot move, no one knows if I am conscious or if only a living body with permanent brain damage lies before them. The machines detected limited activity in the cortex, the doctor says, but because there haven't been even the smallest signs of improvement over time, we can conclude that the patient is brain dead. I see my wife, who signs the organ donation form. I yell, beat at my own body, it's *me*, but no one hears as the machines are turned off. I dream that I wish to drift like a cloud. And it is a cloud that is put on the operating table. It travels into more bodies, into one in the shape of a heart, into another in the shape of kidneys, into a third as lungs. Such vast skies in such tight bodies, I think, so many clouds that search for others at the blue hour, when the furnaces in crematoria are lit, and I wake up like so many others.

When one of the immigrants gathers enough trash, he puts it into a plastic bag and hurls it into treetops in the park. They hang up there in every colour, notes in staves. Sometimes I look at the sky and they swing in the wind like afternoon music, Saint Saëns or Chopin. Now and then one falls, explodes across the flower-beds, and Schnittke plays. One morning I spot one of the immigrants asleep like a treble clef on a branch. The others walk around the tree calling him. I understand nothing but that he sleeps peacefully and deeply. Is he dreaming? Plastic bags sway around him, and in the background, like music behind music, one can identify the pilgrimage of entirely legal clouds.

It was the year they dissolved the Ministry of Weather. The number of hurricanes, heat waves, droughts and floods steadily increased. Talking about the weather, proverbially attributed to the English for centuries, became part of global communication. Weather was everywhere, but meteorologists despaired. Forecasts became ambiguous and slack, cyclones and anticyclones moved in increasingly unpredictable constellations through the lives of people who could no longer tell whether it was a sign of friendship or a sign of hatred when someone addressed them on the subject of the glorious weather.

Perhaps her life will be indelibly marked by the moment when, at four years old, she rode a bus with her mother and in front of her eyes a stranger stole the wallet from her mother's purse. Voice caught in her throat, she went numb and could not say anything, could not move, until the bus door closed again and the stranger's eyes, which held her in complete immobility, vanished behind the clouds, which measure the sky.

She was a little girl with pompoms

She was a little girl with pompoms whose parents and home were taken by war. For one summer she was his sister, until the Red Cross found her distant East German relatives, who took her in. She gropes for her father's hand. An early memory is their only language. Her blue eyes distinguish only light from darkness, but her lacrimal gland works perfectly because of their meeting after so many years.

In 1897, the architect Robert Keldewey came across shards of blue glazed tiles in what is now Iraq and convinced the German emperor to finance the excavation. Shovel after shovel unearthed the broken fragments of Uruk, the city where Gilgamesh's mother, the divine Ninsun, once lived. They were packed in 799 crates, which crossed the ocean so they could be reassembled in Berlin.

In common language: the construction of the destroyed Babylon, the construction of the memory tower, where the little girl with pompoms and my aged father are held captive, the construction of the story of Enkidu's death. The construction of Babylon: to translate a buried memory from a fissure to a fissure, to build a mighty trauma from the missing pieces. The cuneiform tablets in Assyrian, old Babylonian, the gaps in the epic poem about a mortal king, two-thirds deity and one-third human. And the golden lion that guards the Ishtar Gate on the ground floor of the Pergamon Museum.

The little girl with pompoms and her son. Her blindness, his paralysis, the mutual dependence of the disabled. The blind girl doesn't see where she is guiding the immobile man in the wheelchair, through the crowd beneath the spacious dome of the train station.

The construction of the excavated fragments of Uruk took nearly thirty years. As if the bricks were tears, it was necessary to desalinate every fragment in water first, to prepare them to construct a lost unity once again.

A couple of days later, I also arrived in Berlin. Mother, mother, give me your hand, so that we can walk once again through the Ishtar Gate into the breakage.

We go 17 miles on foot

We go 17 miles on foot from Cambridge to Ely. The River Cam meanders towards the north, boats, fields, a few trees. Overgrown bunkers from wars not lived through. A plain. Fences. One must flick open the latch on the gate, pass without hooves over the bars. A metallic clang resounds across the landscape, splits it into a here and a there.

This is my essential baggage. Lorca's poem from *Poet in New York*. A poet is lost in the crowd, which vomits at Coney Island. The vomiting saves them from the dead, who rise from the swamps and threaten the city. The living vomit the names of the dead. Language will save none of those who vomit, but it will guard against the equalisation of both worlds.

Scenes of zombies and werewolves. Nabokov's obsession with lepidopterology, Louis Stevenson, Ovid and Kafka. So many attempts at metamorphosis into some other body. Such a spectacle, so that the very site of transformation wouldn't change. The metamorphosis like a tax to preserve the scenery, the pupation and birth of a butterfly the acts of Zhuangzi's dream.

A poem also pupates, but it's not clear if the cocoon-like enigma will remain in this state forever. Inside it, a message sleeps. Every now and then it forces me to open my mouth for the dentist, wait for some word to flutter from it. A pencil rests against paper, leaves only the barely noticeable diagnosis of the tip.

We've been walking from Cambridge to Ely for six hours. Sinking shoes. For a moment a strong force pulls me into the soil, but its grip weakens. The soil beneath the surface is decisive and definitive, but there is still the difference between the dead and the living. Discarded and lost names, step by step, gulping sandy saliva, poems I once read that have decayed in my memory and unexpectedly reemerge. Sometimes they are bright butterflies that land on the naked shoulders of my beloved, sometimes barely noticeable signs on the horizon. They sail closer. No, they aren't masts, *son los cementerios, lo sé, son los cementerios.*

Here is just one of the entrances

Here is just one of the entrances. During stolen hours and rainy days, darkness covers me in a buzzing. A face is cooled by a flame, which finishes what it started. I'm only a gathering of thoughts, a trembling of tiny wings, a fleeting attempt to attach a body to a windy crossroads. Here is just one of the exits. Here is where I break a stick off of silence, prod the beehive.

Nature knows that the colour of pain is green. It doesn't know the concept of consolation and it buds from dry stumps and cracks in the asphalt, from rotten leaves in the gutter and the contact of the ground. Three bears frozen mid-fall on a canvas by Walton Ford. Three bears chased up a tree by farmers, who lit a fire below. Three bear cubs. The first calls me a hunter. The second calls me a fall. The third calls me a brother. On the canvas they are frozen mid-fall. It is I who plummet in front of the canvas.

A biting stick, pushed between the patient's teeth during a surgery without anaesthesia. I write all night, strike everything in the next draft until it hurts. My teeth are getting looser. Why does the stick rest? Where do the letters fall out? And anyway, who are you?

In an unfortunately lost note for the report from the Siberian expedition in 1829, Alexander von Humboldt reports on the Tudara tribe. The savages evidently created a unique form of coexistence with the East Siberian brown bear, otherwise hostile towards men. Both were gatherers, loners and highly unapproachable. The Tudara did not know the uses of language. Basic communication was established through an incomprehensible code of signs with no apparent structure or consistency. Their, at least in Humboldt's view, incomprehensible thinking (*Undenken*, notes Humboldt) acquired the outline of logic and sense only in a peculiar dialogue with bears. They responded to the occasional bear roar with a distinctive kind of muffled singing, which recalled, more than anything else, the buzzing hive of wild bees.

It's always possible to interpret the real as the exorcist of pain from words. Unresponsive, with the calloused skin of invented meanings, but only apparently. Oh, just whip them, break them, put them on the rack, roll them through solitary confinement. Everything is only deception. No shot into the temple of a revolutionary, no rusty nail deep in the palms of a martyr will do. They must be concealed with a trick, comprehended by the unthinkable, tolerated fearfully like plankton. What has happened will happen time and again, but as if in a broken mirror. Inside it a rock lies motionless for 36 years. But that's enough for a new body to grow from the green stains.

The smell of rotting logs

The smell of rotting logs, little signs that explain the view. The sentences read *toredo navalis*, worms in seawater that chew through the wood in which they live. But there is little salt in these seas, so sentences echo more quietly in the ears of the drowning.

I read, but this isn't an explanation. Words position themselves in space like a ship under construction. The verb runs from bow to stern, still no propeller, but there are already lions' heads, which will sink into the water once again, like 382 years ago, at the maiden voyage. And the water will be what you live, what we live, what of us, scattered in tiny holes in the wood, lives.

I read, but this isn't an explanation: None of the Vasa skeletons can be identified by name. The skeletons hauled to the surface were marked in the order of their discovery with letters based on a Swedish radio code. The skeleton of male stranger A became Adam, the skeleton of female stranger B became Beata.

For two thousand years, the teeth sown in the soil grew at the top of a cliff. As if the 59 teeth of 59 individuals were transformed into a community only through the constellation of their placement in the shape of a ship's hull. I walk among the broken names speaking of rocky massifs lighter than clouds. Ales Stenar. My departure is my cenotaph.

In the last hall in the Natural History Museum in Götenborg is the only stuffed blue whale in the world. Its skeleton is exhibited beside it. In the old days there was a café inside the whale. It was closed down after a naked couple were caught in the hull.

Postscript: In the wall of the museum in this poem, traces

of the hole are still visible. They had to make the hole, so in the penultimate verse they brought in a cloud shaped like a whale, and in the last one left the imprint of a ship in the sky.

She spends her afternoons sitting

She spends her afternoons sitting on the edge of a large double bed in which she has slept alone for twenty years. She buries her face in the palms of her hands. In surges of memories she travels to her childhood, walks from the house to the barn, cracks open the door. In the semi-darkness, the muddy soles of her father's shoes gradually become visible, slowly swinging like a weight one metre above the ground.

Our religion is based on our faith in apoptosis, cell death. Without external influences or environmental changes, the cells are predestined to self-destruction. Their highest law, that their time is strictly determined. That there is *that* time. They are dying in my knee, but I still run. In my left eye, a graveyard. Writing, writing, the death of benumbed words. But how far does the analogy go? Isn't it too soon for every organism, including a man, to be declared a letter? And what about single-celled protozoa, which destroy themselves in the process of division? Death without a corpse, a poem without characters, a foot pushes off the ground, an eye closes in a sudden gust of wind.

I remember that, as a child, I always had to stay quiet when a funeral procession marched through the village with a coffin. My grandmother and grandfather stood behind the curtain, counted the mourners and altar boys, verified which villagers had attended the funeral. It would be inappropriate if passers-by noticed that they were being watched, heard that someone from the outside had intruded on their ceremony. I remember a special sense of space always began to prevail in the house after they'd all gone. As if the mourners had not trudged down the street towards the cemetery, but had left through an invisible door in the bedroom. It was closed and the space was now pregnant from the funeral.

Beneath the Pont Mirabeau, the Seine continues to erase those of us who remain. The alleged place of voluntary death does not coincide with a magnificent view of Parisian rooftops. Too melodramatic a place, too theatrical an exit. The passage is so narrow and dim that the dead could wrap themselves in it. The passage is no more, so one must exit through the wall there, where there are no more metaphors, no analogies, a persistent obliteration by days and the Seine. Which in the poem remains as *I* do, a place without a place, a wall of water that pushes away the living and the dead.

They were breezy days. The wind broke the geraniums on the balcony before we moved them into the house, it rolled leaves, plastic bags and other trash, danced with the tops of horse chestnuts and apple trees, bent cypresses. If someone walked down the street alone, furtively tilted into the pummelling wind, he held on to his hat or coat collar, as if his hands belonged to another. Curtains simultaneously concealed and exposed him. The finely embroidered, vertical surface of the river called into question *here* and *there*.

With a cheek pressed

With a cheek pressed against the car window. For a moment I see a man running across a field. It is January 20, even though it is November 15. I meet myself, some me, some him, some *disappearing me* in the encounter. There is no return, like a body that doesn't return from anesthesia, or someone who is no longer missed after years of travel. Only some man who runs, with no name and with no story to attribute to him. Some last time. The field where he ran is no longer there, only a genealogy of the heirs of the field. The diagnosis, the unearthing that cuts into the face.

Embodied experience when you read this. The body takes everything. The territory of definitions grafted onto the skin. I disappear into my own prior future. I will die obliterated by a multiplicity of connections.

We went as far as possible from Via Dolorosa, over the rooftops of the city. His gaze caught on the barbed wire that separated houses and walls. He could place it precisely, the year and location of the first production, Austin, Texas, 1936. Years ago, he had bought a more extensive collection, some 80 different specimens, which he had patiently supplemented ever since. There are only some 120 different specimens of barbed wire, all the rest are derivations, he said as we descended towards the Gethsemane garden and eight olive trees, guarded by the wire. To be awake in language. To sleep peacefully among stitches.

I cannot find it in Slovenian lexicons between (h)endeca-syllable and endorphins. Perhaps all biology is local. In such moments, the word *minority* in every language is written in Slovenian. Although it's a common everyday occurrence in my culture: *endocannibalism*. The embodiment of the soul of the dead in the bodies of their living descendants. The separation of the soul from the body of the dead.

I dream of how fog withdraws from the forest at daybreak. It moves like a razor between the treetops, and only later, when it dawns, do I see the fire devouring the forest. A firing squad marches up the hill in tight rows. The clarity of scorched earth lingers. My parents' house is at the top of the hill. A little while longer and it is swallowed by flame and day.

Above the red button it says

Above the red button it says *poussez ici*. You press and two old women, who sit inside a small box on the wall and drink tea, shake their mandibles. Automatons. Automatons. Some mechanism propels the visitors of *Musée des automates et de la magie* deeper through the catacombs. As if they stepped beneath the arches of some incessantly dividing question. And there is the master of magic, Houdini with his mustache, body floating above his hands, unclasped chains around a hypnotised beauty and a magic hat. Less and less oxygen and more and more staring eyes, although only the effects of language are visible, sometimes levers and cogs, never a finger, which presses a button so you will speak.

At one in the morning, he leans over and says *res publica academia* to the dark-skinned porter at *École normale supérieure*. His father always blamed himself for not speaking to the German teacher he met near the bridge from which he intended to commit suicide. Mao always blamed himself for the Cultural Revolution not having sufficiently purged the French Maoists. The French Maoists blamed themselves for not abolishing the Latin lectures of their father. The son blamed himself for enduring the theft by the Maoist philosophers, who stole Prometheus' lighter from the French poet's pocket. *Res publica academia*. The tireless babble of a fountain on an August night. The busts of the members of this strange society on the four walls around the inner courtyard of golden Ernests. Pascal, who reproached the newcomer for not writing more sublimely, Montaigne, who reproached the newcomer for not writing more independently, Rousseau, who reproached the newcomer for not writing more revolutionarily, Proust, who reproached the newcomer for not writing his shibboleth more like a hermit.

They tighten the early morning moisture. Voices carry the nails and leave them hanging in the air, the sounds of banging pipes and drills boring. Sometimes one of them falls off a ladder, his scream leaves a shaft in the middle of sentence construction. Long ago, they shaded the windows. But a wall doesn't grow only next to a wall, wall to wall. Their hammers and wires, shelves and weldings, grow through a window and into a room, tightening the drops that fall from a pipe and the little movements of the suits in a closet. They have tightened my left middle ear, attached my eyelids to my cheeks, evaporated my hand with a cheap trick. I can no longer move. Dates have fastened me. At the same time, I am prey to an evil spell. I sense that they drilled through to my tongue.

Never again will I see the first word nor the last subjects of the sentence, whose conjunction I've become, never the tenses where there's this never.

As if I were scouring a book of false biographies that might have been written by someone under the pseudonym of my name. The skyscraper in Montparnasse casts a long shadow over the graves. I cannot find the aged Trilce, only trash hidden behind tombstones. Robert-Houdin. To search. To be found in loss. Is it an encounter if we are sought out by a poem? In what time, with which date is the word stamped when it stands against time again and again? Before the book closes me, instead of the magic show ending at the farewell poem, there is always a black button. Under it the aged clockmaker for the Marabouts added: *poussez ici.*

Still, when I turn the corner

Still, when I turn the corner of Slovenska and Šubičeva Streets, he is standing there, like years ago when I last saw him. He embraced me in farewell and held me longer than usual; and he is still standing and holding me there, in a time that increasingly belongs only to me. All the passers-by have died in my memories, the sky blurred first, then the date, then the season, the sycamores have sprouted leaves and the shadows of their trunks have vanished. Which trunks? No taxi reflects off the display window any more. No display window and no monument to a martyr of the revolution. He's still holding me, I hold him, I am increasingly this holding, held in time. The poetics of amputation.

Fortunately, I have no memory. There are pictures from what we call the past, certainly, but what about memory? Do I remember a memory I used to intentionally forget or falsify something? At most I remember the day that never happened when, as a child, I played with two broken toy cars on the living room carpet, and the toy cars became aeroplanes, and the aeroplanes became two large drops of water. They fell into the sea. Who says I sprinkled the carpet with salt? What binds me to what memories designate is the inevitable and detailed precision mechanics of daydreaming.

Does a poem emerge finished, like Athena from Zeus' skull? Yet we forget about the headache of the greatest of gods. About the destabilisation of everything that tells us what we are. About the crucifixion, which so brutally stifled the shuffling of the golden sandals of the immortals on Olympus. I ask, I shout into the eons, I mutter in a muffled voice: do I really need a theology of the pencil in order to write?

I read books about the architecture of hoarfrost, studied large atlases about the desires of flowering plants, small volumes of debates about the metallurgy of dead languages, dusty scrolls about the genetics of the east wind, ambiguous tracts on the theosophy of spruces, the cosmology of pain. Essays on chemothanatology, sociogulagology, experimental nosology, exodology, escapology covered my body, which shivered in light sleep and couldn't determine if, in a dream, it was cooled by hellfire or warmed by angelic coolness.

My universities were buried with the bones of the murdered, my lecture halls were always filled with solitude and silent mornings, my lessons were cruel beatings, losses and betrayals. When I registered for an exam, I'd already failed, because I didn't know what to write in the column 'name'. Save me, wise men of the academies, help me, professorial gentlemen, every moment they take from me the gaze that watches them.

After only half an hour

After only half an hour of the film, even before the first drop of blood, I cannot endure any more suspense, turn off the television, go to bed. The horror proliferates in sleep then even in wakefulness, executioners and victims, intimate persons, but not from my life. From where? What had I done in one of my pasts to be so vulnerable, what have they done to my soul? To my perforated, porous soul.

It isn't clear who invented the stethoscope, but it's obvious that the device mimics the ear of a baby pressing against the uterus from within. We grew in the land of sounds, were raised by the murmur of blood flow, of food digesting, skin tightening, bones cracking. At the beginning I saw the cosmos with my ears. Such a terror of light, birth. Such a fall into a transitory state of phantasms and illusions, from which we will return only after a long and noisy battle. But to what? Where?

It's easy to be smart about the soul, says the professor. Plato's dualism and the soul of the Early Church Fathers. A spirit, which rises from the body and observes it like a newly finished drawing, gazes at William Blake. The soul of hands and the soul of technology. The soul of sewing machines, the soul of a diving bell, and the soul of a nuclear plant. Some people, the professor says, believe not only that a soul resides in every termite and blade of grass, but also that the soul is everything that surrounds everything, and that we are only a foreign body in the soul. That there are only two possibilities. First, that we will destroy everything, second, that the soul will consume us and metabolise us into itself.

A child's fear of the darkness under the stairs. Any moment, a hand will burst through the stairs out of the gloom, grab my foot and drag me into the dark. I needed 36 years to associate this fear with my name, Aleš, Alessio, a self-outcast and urban hermit who lived and died unidentified under the stairway of his own house. My fear before this, that a hand drags me into my name, that I crash into the darkness of the language that I am.

It's easy to be smart about the soul. These words are increasingly muffled. It's snowing. The professor is dead. The professor is alive. The snow brings peace to the holes in his soul. Snow is skin that equally covers the departing and the deceased, stretches a membrane that time chimes against. There, where I come from, people put on masks to chase away the snow, hanging insatiable tongues, warty noses, horns and feathery ears. They trudge across a landscape that their movement simultaneously creates. When they remove the masks, the prospect of my return stitches up the lacerations of spring.

Who mediates for you?

Who mediates for you? A wandering cloud stops embodying the sky time and again. Although the tufts of hair, limbs, and individual bodies of these foamy worlds seem for a moment inevitably solid in the blue. Zephyrs break up the mist in the streets. Four half of six. Stations, terminals, platforms and morgues, saturated with waiting.

October winks. The auditory hallucinations of the ocean breeze still hum around his dirty ears. On the avenue, dandruff covertly falls onto the shoulders of a man who taps a cigarette onto fallen leaves and calculates traffic connections. So many possibilities, so many variables, so many sums, but they all lead to Raron.

Seven fifteen to one-eighth. I travel like the blue between clouds. I am, therefore I dicker, a pedologist between strata. Volatile I and his better double, Mister Like. Mister? Like a foetus in formaldehyde.

We lay one another in encyclopedias and urns. I also wear a little time. A little onion, which blunt fingers spasmodically squeeze in the perforated pocket in my coat. Will it cry out, my little counting rhyme without a centre and without assistance?

I travel through a delineated everywhere and everywhere the mystery of the Arabic number zero. The sum of zero and negative sky is zero. The sum of zero and positive soil is zero. The sum of zero and zero is, more and more, me.

A German Shepherd beside a girl

A German Shepherd beside a girl in a black-and-white photograph with a blurred background on the northern wall of your writing room above the garage next to the house beside the cemetery. This is how my language works. The space of a finger next to the space of a palm next to the space of a forearm next to the space of an upper arm next to the space of a shoulder joint next to the space of a right lung in the space of a torso. Individual words live for themselves alone, they're an autonomous territory. Like the inhabitants of mountain farms they form a body only during holidays and wars. And your language? Interdependence and reciprocity. Words like the types of shells that have washed up on the shore of the bay near your house (in my language). They adhere to one another, rely on a strength that relies on them. *Crepidula fornicada*, you say and continue to translate. You say that one must seize words, that words hold themselves when you carry them from language to language. Then we talk about the maniraptors, dinosaurs that, 140 million years ago, developed a flexible joint in their forelimbs, allowing them to grab and hold. *Deinocheirus mirificus* in the American Museum of Natural History in New York, enormous arms, found in Mongolia.

Bushes grow between the house and the cemetery. In a little while, they will lose their last leaves. Tombstones are already visible from the veranda. Numerous small flags by the graves. Flags in my language, memorial plaques in yours. They mark the graves of soldiers. Some fell in past wars, others in wars that pass like the bright red leaves on bushes. An increasingly porous boundary.

I dream a word, lose it the moment I wake. I don't understand it in dreams, the word in your language. You try to explain again and again. It doesn't work. The word won't go into my language. You grab a bottle, point at the cork.

You keep explaining. In a language without words, you say, in a language dreamily mute, you say that this word doesn't let one side into the other, that it's so introverted it doesn't let even a single word's impermeability, mine, yours, anyone's words, cross to the other side.

Complete darkness when we reach the shore. A footstep sinks gently, but it's too dark for the prints to be visible. The smell of seaweed. It rustles when I walk on it. As if, dried out, it still possessed a living language that feeds on random steps. In the gloom we nearly bump into two fishermen, their rods protruding like antennae towards the absence of stars. On our way back, one of them bends. We stand and stare at the watch glimmering on the wrist of the fisherman as he reels in the line, a trace on the calm surface of the darkness, the gills of the word *hlastač* in my language, pulsing in a frantic struggle, the gills of the word *snapper*, which the other fisherman says in yours.

We're very late. Only three pages of text, but the translation has dragged on. Until the last, you dragged meanings out of sentences, opened the dictionary, examined the possibilities for a solution. Around the corner you turn down the street that leads through the cemetery. The difference between my and your languages is that my language doesn't allow cars to drive across the cemetery, past the graves, between the sixth and seventh row, towards the south exit. Even less does it allow the sentence, which you speak in your language and which I inadequately translate, just as we translate dreams: *Across the cemetery, I'll safely drive you home*.

The ancient Roman walls

The ancient Roman walls. *Opus mixtum*. Still some *still*. It still stands, like some dental prosthesis displaying an impression that has just been consumed by time. A washed-off stone, a porous brick – here, no century has broken all its teeth, ground down its tongue. It is upright, grey on red, where hunger sticks in the throat and hours smell of migratory birds.

I still skip over names, as if they were stairs, clouds dripping through my hair, still *still*, tattooed beneath the liver, branded on the kidneys, stitched beneath the Adam's apple, which renounces Paradise and devours, ah, devours.

A silent witness of how everything diminishes in abundance, of how in my body nostrils leak air and shoulders sink, of how, more and more, the body has collapsed as if whipped onward, onward, through ever smaller doors, a calculating rebel, a mangy revolutionary, a subversive for three bugs, a charlatan of a narrow slice of the world.

It still surpasses a gnat, is still faster than the leaves that fall on an August morning. Still, I say, still, with bones between screws and a gnawed-on wallet, with glassware in the mouth and a bladder filled with jewels. Still, I say, for thirty-six years it has left through the pores in the skin. Not sweat, but the contraction that comes without shots and trumpets, without biopsies and solemn ceremonies, quietly like the faded stamp on still another misplaced document.

Like bark, I fall off myself. I let a palisade grow around me to protect me from the barbarians. When I cough, a branched-out territory trembles like a tree. Still, the gold scarab gnaws. Its jaws have crushed stubbornness and misfortune. Its jaws, high in the trunk, have split my vocal chords. Its jaws in my jaws. Quickly, quickly, doctor sir, take an impression of the gap, extract the gold tooth from the babbling mouth of the dead before it cries out still. Hurry, dear doctor, as long as there's still a little palate.

The closer the deadline

The closer the deadline, the more nervously I move piles of scrawled-on paper and books around the apartment. Castles of sand. Every hour there's a larger wave, and the horizon, lurking behind the English term *deadline*, is more and more tangible.

A captive of circling thoughts and helplessness. To relax, I jog up Golovec. At first my legs won't obey, but then the forest embraces me with its oxygen. I'm jogging uphill, I know the path by heart, it will curve three more times and disappear before I see the crest dipping where the word *path* descends, limping. Like the silhouette of a woman in a night window, a view of Barje marsh opens up before me.

Years ago there were only swampy fields and meadows, cut through by canals, full of stagnant water. Then they were filled, asphalted, and shopping centres appeared as if they'd fallen from the saddlebags of fugitive gods. More and more people. But soon the roads wrinkle, the fissures in the asphalt start signing the undercarriages of cars. The swamp returns without megaphones and spectacles, as grim as the flight of a raven over an empty car park.

I read the sentence 'someone speaks from the belly of the word'. Read literally, someone speaks from the belly, that of the word that has consumed its own speaker. He's swallowed in the belly of the word, speaking simultaneously. Inside and outside intertwine, are an intersection beyond the imaginable. Where does the mutilation of thought come from, so that I believe a word literally but miss a simple description of someone who, mouth closed, says *Noah, you are a fish. I'm a fish?*

They all fulfil their assignments, only I apologise. Some opportunity is thus closed, some other horizon emerges, and with it, other seas. I sit stiffly, almost paralyzed, and listen to the presentations. I close my eyes and see the shadow of the woman in the night window again. She is illuminated only by a candle, which will burn out at any moment. The window opens and before me is a wave, which rises from the depths of the earth and overcomes me, returning what was made from sand back to sand.

Of all the healers

Of all the healers he trusted only the one who broke into his dreams to meet with his pasts, with the sames within him that were his future. In a little while he will fall into their shadow. In front of the window of a socialist apartment building, the crown of a chestnut tree, daylight coming to an end. A modest interior, a table for one, for two.

It remains a mystery how the same is simultaneously something else, what we reluctantly carry stubbornly enters us and replaces us more and more. Shamanic transformations, the wise man's stone, conifers in bloom, a babble that is suddenly a poem foreseen in the distance, Guaya and Quil, Baba Yaga, Girl. Transformations, falls, wanderings. What is visible when the invisible is always our final determination? What is the future if we reproduce with letters, vegetative?

It isn't clear if the cawing of crows, usually three or four consecutive calls, but also tapping and snapping, represents a more complex language. But various species from the *Corvidae* family, as Linnaeus classified crows, can mimic the human voice. A crow that speaks poetry is the most obvious example of assigning the characteristics of a crow to man, a phenomenon called *corvumorphosis* in literary science.

We remained alone. Shepherds, each herding his flock of silence through a dark space. His face goes white from chemotherapy. His face is the other same. After growing in him undetected for seventy-five years, he now presses the other same face from within, so his own cheek becomes more and more present in vanishing. He turns, but does not click on the light. As if, following the traces of an erased path, he'd gone too far. From there the word returns through the darkness. Barefoot and without a body, the voice walks behind the sheep. Soft as wool, it moves through the kitchen. The darkness is vast, and the path travelled is as small as an orange, another planet on the sideboard.

That he's happy as never before in his life, he says into the silence. That he truly feels love, a hoarse voice after a sheer silence. As if it had stepped off a cliff into the arms of the abyss, the voice says that it loves, loves and is loved. Under the window, the wind sways the canopy in the night, unravels its leaves, and all the crows from the sky.

I've scattered my body

I've scattered my body. My knee in the Puszta. My aortas under the sleeping vicugnas. My eyeballs under second class seats in German trains. My cracking bones at the sites of transit airports and random histories. Right palm in more hands than I can recall. And my left in the pockets of trousers taken apart by long-dead moths.

When will I be ready? In the quiet night, I crept out of myself, and while the death knell sang I ate the remains of what I'd shed. My only food: the error of repetition. Here are grapes of Dionysius and ripe berries, which burst into a dismembered body in the face of terror, that of a smiling god. I cannot forget that I've scattered my throat in the Poetoviona and that oblivion is my necessary dessert after starving.

It's only the third stanza, but I already resist being disgusted with the first-person narrative. But how else to grant the body an instinctive emotional intelligence (or rather the logic of lunacy?), which travels across time and joins a pale cheekbone from Pontus with a crooked nose from Ravenna with a mutilated arm from Voronezh with a slender breastbone from Bukovina with an ear from Laz with a rib that, in this place, joins with this place, for an unknown, presumably never-born moment?

Tell me when I'll be ready. The maritime metaphor is loaded to the brim, the plumb is submerged, the masts creak impatiently and the deck is strewn with supplies and valuables and animal specimens of all kinds. Swaying beneath the deck are chests overflowing with symbols, which percolate from riddle to riddle. At least tell me in some incomprehensible language, is there any chance of survival in the face of wayward verbs, decomposing nouns, prepositions as porous as the night?

It always dawns late in January. In the distance, highway noise and an unusually cheerful warbling. The echo of footsteps crossing the Mathematical Bridge. I've asked enough in my sleep and am no longer hungry. It's light enough for me to hear the grass growing from my skin and to feel the roots of the wild thorn across my forehead. I forget. My only ally is a lie and my last betrayer is dust.

The word BARE.
Everyone
Exposed
To his
Only language.
More silent
Than bare.
More a place
Than its
Exchangeable name.
More movement
Through the possibility
Of a place
That negates
Itself
In its creation.
Movement.
A silhouette
That
Gradually
Retreats
To the corner
Of a bedroom
In a house
That has not yet
Been built
On the edge
Of a town
That has not yet
Been
Founded.
A meadow.
But the word
GRASS
Does not grow.
Bare soil.
Everyone
Buried in it.

Everyone dusty.
Everyone
Dust among dust.
With a face
To the sky.
It starts to rain.
The bare word
Slowly sinks in
The dug-up mud.
A body that
Disappears into
A quotation.

The word BUT,
A newborn,
Just a letter
But already a but,
A place of exception
Where thought
Chips off
Into contradiction.
Drop by drop
The river makes
A turn,
None
Are broken.
The lost
Sovereignty
Opens
A travelling
Wound.
An exhale
Lays
The word ARNICA
Across the gaping
Li   ne,
Simultaneously
Finds
And loses
Language.
The word
Does not heal it,
Only veils.
Inhale.
Though not even
Conceived,
Everything is already
Complete.
The river
Still flows and
Arnica still blooms

In that place
Where wound
After wound
Drips
Through time
Into its own
Opposite.
The word BUT.
But there is
No time.

The word EATS
Time,
In which
It has meaning.
Fangs
Tear,
Molars
Grind
Milliseconds,
Three, two,
During which
A syllable
Sighs,
And between
The time of the word
And the time
When
A word
Is devoured,
An opportunity
Springs forth.
Two, one,
And the word
That almost
Was
Already will be.
Yes yes.
A word traces
A word
About time,
Presses it into
Nonsense,
Grabs it by
The throat,
Punctures.
After millennia
Of gluttony,
Increasingly

Swollen
Stomachs
Walk
In front of the smallest
Conjunctions,
Ornamental
Adjectives,
Auxiliary
Verbs.
Fattened
Words,
Dictatorship,
Devaluation,
Dilettantism
Lounge
Between columns.
Zero,
One, zero,
And chomp they go,
Already grabbing,
Ravenous
To the last
Syllable,
Always
On the hunt,
In order to snap
At an utterly
Famished
Meaning.
The transparent skin
Splits,
Time's wrapping
Around the thought
Vanishes
Into another
Word
Starved
Into timelessness,

The same as
Its obese
Predecessor
With its prepredecessor,
The same as
The coming
Word,
The glutton
Frays,
Chews,
Swallows.
Not every
Wordivorous
Word
Is carnivorous.
But each
One has
An insatiable
Word-for-word
Appetite.

The word END
At all ends
And places
So you
Become more and more
An archive.
The word END,
The word UNREADY,
An incision that requires
Trust.
Without a trace,
Like drowning
In a vanishing sentence
During
Quiet lovemaking.
The end of a poem.
Not a place,
Indeterminacy,
A body,
Not mine
Not yours,
The body of a relic.
It pierces us
Like a needle,
Like the word NEEDLE.
It sewed nothing,
Unstitched nothing.
The word pricks,
The body moans,
Extends a tongue,
Though nothing
Happens,
Everything
Has once again
Concluded.
From an end
Two hands
Grow.

A body,
Everywhere
Open
On all sides
Of a place
That only
Can be
Circumvented,
A name
That is missing,
Every beginning
Abolished.

The word FOLDS
An image
Over an image.
Meaning
Doesn't increase.
Only the terror
Of coincidences
Is assessable enough
And the edges
More clearly
Marked
By paradoxes.
Another today
Folds itself
Into the word ONCE
And into the word
That does not see.
Concealment
Is an axiom.
Masters of origami
Are known
To hide
Between their own
Fingers
Without stopping
Their time-consuming
Task.
Like the hands
Fold
Paper,
Time
Folds
Words.
Little birds, little ships,
Hats made from
Old magazines
Are massacres,
Epidemics.

A cataclysm folded over
A motorcyclysm.
A surreal
Cynicism?
Image over
Image.
Memory
Folds you
Into the indifferent
Word ONCE
And the word
That is not visible.

The word HERE,
The heaviest word,
It weighs more
Than a grammar
And vocabulary
Full of elephants.
Here is a place,
An over-saturated
Crossroads
Of dead ends.
The word HERE
Puts
The word JUNGLE in it.
In it, the word ELEPHANT,
Which breaks into it.
The word is nearly
Empty.
Only a hole
Inside a hole
Inside
Emptiness.
A mouth without lips,
Without a throat,
Swallowing a word.
The word HERE,
A word where
Once upon a time
The word ELEPHANT
Stretched out its trunk.
Even though the hole
Does not mark
The place of disappearance.
There was something.
There isn't something any more.
Some once upon a time,
The lightness with
Which it breaks into
A mouth that rattles

One more time,
But it isn't dying,
You think,
And this thought
Breaks into
The question
About the disappearance of death.
And the question breaks
Into the objection NO,
NO into the argument
About the arrival of death,
Which has no
Here of its own;
It arrives with
Its own unplaces.
Enter,
You absent guest,
Leave,
You unreadable trace,
Still
In search of
A world
For a place,
Which it carries
With itself.

The word HOLE.
And a hole
In the word.
You crawl
Into it,
In darkness
The hesitation of waterdrops.
You are turned over to
Its I Ching
Within unknown
Limitations.
A deadly persistence.
Bent into
The beginning, you wait
For the skin
That grows
Between the syllables
On your feet,
For the body
To become transparent
And dull.
You try.
Nothing.
You don't move.
You are the breath
That no one
Warms up.
You don't know
When
An icy
Sappho's finger
Will place
A seed
Under your tongue.
A shaft
Of light
Sprouts,
Suddenly

A tree
Grows inside
The word HOLE.
Its leaves knock
Against you,
It is fertilised,
Trunks grow
In the word
HOLE,
It is more and more
Light
And less and less
Hole.
With atrophying
Sight
You are entangled
In treetops,
Tendrils
And ferns
And vines
Hatch you.
There is no echo
In such
Dense
Woods.
Only the dull
Sound of patter
On stones.
Only a tiny
Hole,
A small
Crack.
You dig
Into it.
You don't know
That a seed already
Sprouts under
Your tongue,

Expels you
From secure
Darkness.

The word LIMPS.
It sniffs,
Still a word.
Still a word still.
Better one that limps
Than
One that
Wanders.
A stray with
A bitten-off tail.
As if
The injury
Weren't enough,
As if there were
Still still,
It still always
Needs
The lack of a tail
For this
Still, which sniffs
For the lack.
As if this
Still still
Wanted.
It goes into.
Still into.
And into
The command
You still go,
Put on its
Fur,
Organise its
Internal organs,
Lungs,
Pancreas,
Still more and more
Hidden in
Its forehead,

Twice
Pierce
The snout
Of the word STILL,
Inhale
Every syllable
And
Howl.
If you
Lie down
In the stomach
Of the word
Like a gnawed
Bone, you'll
Howl inwards,
Sniff ahead,
Follow
The illusion of landscapes
And yards
Without a reason,
Without a leash.

The word MISSING.
Dull as
The guilt of a hoe
Because it has split
The clod.
Like brothers,
Each on his own
Side of the stretcher.
Like the state of the world
And funeral fashion
The year before last.
The word MISSING.
Only herself.
Only himself.
Only itself.
The imprints of shoes
Arrange themselves,
Letters around
An open
Mouth in the earth.
Wordlessly
We feed them.
Our insatiable
Soil
Is permanently newborn.
It doesn't grow.
It only beckons
Her to herself,
Him to himself,
It to itself.
We feed them
Language.
Stuff them
With the word MISSING.
Increasingly alone,
We are missing
Among the words
Of the perfect dictionary.

The word NEAR.
A word that wants
To expand the body.
To embrace until
Annihilation.
A word that wants
To be near,
To be more,
To be where
A word gives up.
Someone hears
Someone else gasp
In his name,
Rips him
From the dictionary.
Someone smells
Someone else's fear
In their hair.
He burns grass.
Someone tastes lamentation
With his fingernails.
Drools on an envelope.
The word NEAR.
A word that wants
From someone
Who is someone
To be,
To be
More and more a word
That cannot
Fall asleep
In any other
Words,
A word
That cannot
Be
Nobody.

The word NO
Leaning on
Another.
You drill
Small holes into it,
Peer through them
To the other side.
Fill them
With slightly twisted
Meanings.
You wait
And everything is
Waiting
For you.
Leaning on
Your helplessness,
This waiting stands
In the middle of days,
Hidden,
How leaning bodies
Hide each other.
It's easy
To avoid
Opposites
With words.
Later
The word
You're leaning on
Moves,
Leans through you,
Your own NO
Pierces you
Without a wound.
No shadow
No dusk.
A magic trick.
Hocus.
Pocus.

An evergreen
Wall.

The word PASS.
A word in
Sandals,
Torn
From nowhere roads.
It has to go through you.
Even before
It drapes itself
With your voice,
The sagging
Space
Settles.
You don't know
Where it must go,
But your
Dedicated ignorance
Inside a wallet
Is the only
Luggage
Light enough
To pass over
The mountain of silence.
Beneath it
They are smuggling
The dead.
Above it
The white shadows
Of clouds.
They only move over it
When you say
The names
Of the souls.

The word PFFF
Through the world.
Wordless.
Bodiless.
A movement of hands
Without hands.
The movement itself
Just a breath
In the ear.
Without a where,
Without a what.
An eye into
No place.
Where there is no ahead.
Where there is no back.
Only a little PFFF
On a strange path
That has no importance
And makes no sense,
Not the feel of things,
Nor the naming of days.
Not a lament
And not a shout.
A nothing
From no one
To nobody.
A jackanape,
The word PFFF.
A nothing
That exists.
But without words.
And without silence.
An exhalation
Without a mouth.
A sound
Without a voice.
A world
Without a world.

A nothing,
A PFFF,
Without origin
And without audience.

The word SAVES
The word.
The body
Does not
Save the body.
The word
Saves
Saving
But is not
Salvation.
The body
Is not
Saved,
But it saves.
The word is not
Saved
And is not
The body.
The body and
The word,
The word is not
The body.
Sometimes
The body
Wants
To be
A word.
An unsolved
Riddle.
Sometimes the body
Becomes
The word.
The word
Never
Becomes
The body,
But it
Needs the body

To save
Words.
The body needs the word
For
Informing
Other
Bodies.
The word
Needs
The body
For
Saving
The word,
Which
Tells
Other
Bodies
There is no
Salvation.
Both,
The body and
The word,
Will be
Saved,
But not in
Words
Nor in
Bodies,
Says the word.
The body
Believes it.
It is easier
To believe
With
Words,
With which
It believes
It will not be

Saved,
Than to believe
Without
Words.
And what
Belief
Would that
Be,
Belief
Of bodies,
Which does not
Save
Even
One
Single
Word
For
Salvation.
The word saves
The word, in
Which
The body
Does not
Believe.
Without the body
Not even
The word
Would
Believe in
The salvation
That saves
It.

The word SEEDS.
A word that
Spills
Out of the cracks
Of a cypress cone
When you strike,
When, without thinking, while
Passing by,
You strike
A signpost
With the cone
In your palm,
When it
Spills
Into your palm.
So much language,
It's hard
To plant,
Hard
To grow
In the middle of asphalt
And crossroads
And dead ends
The small word
TREE,
Near
Another,
Smaller
Word TREE,
Just sown
Seedy word,
And yet another and
Another,
Until they
Expel,
Until they
Overgrow
The word CLEARING.

When you write it down,
You disappear
Into
A wood.

The word SULLIES
Memory.
Love
Sullies
Life.
Darkness gets
Sullied
By day,
Washes itself,
Becomes night again.
A word steps
Over fire sites
And places
That will burn,
Sullies
What man is.
Impossible to wash clean.
What is exterminated
Sullies
Man.
Man cannot
Be clean
Though sometimes he tries.
The mouth
Gets sullied
By food.
Earth
Gets sullied
By footsteps.
What man was
Gets sullied by
What he missed out on being.
The word sullies
Memory.
Inside his body
A man
Hides
Another man

When darkness
Starts to fall.

The word TATTERS.
Weathered pieces
Of old
Melodies,
Quotations,
Folded
Inside the pockets
Of new, oh,
Always new
Words.
They get worn out.
Destroyed by
Moths,
Revolutions,
Poets.
A still
Unspoken
Noun
Of action
Of future
Verb tense
Is already mending.
Like the impression
Of bodies
In the soil,
A word
Decays
In the powerlessness
Of space,
The shape of a word,
Never definitively
Remembered,
Definitively
Saved language.
Someone takes a step.
Some nobody
Who will
Once again

Mend
The echoes
Of faded footsteps
Into departure.
This tomorrow's WHEN
Without utopia
And place
Is the song
Of today's
Dissolution.

The word WAITING
Under the harrow.
The earth is waiting
For the grain
To be sown.
It sprouts.
The wheat is waiting
For the moons.
Grinding
The flour for weeks
For the yeast.
One, two days
And the mouth
Goes back on its word.
A musty gold coin
In the bread.
The teeth
Stop grinding
For a moment.
The hidden
Shadow of a mountain
Reveals the field.
It is a secret
Why
The waiting is slower
For the fall
Into silence
As one
Climbs up
The word.
Hungry and thirsty,
It arrives
Unannounced.
Its story
About its adventures
Is food
For the wind.

The word WALKS.
Through suburbs,
Sleeves,
Favours.
But a camel
Is needed
To pass
Through the ear
Of a needle.
The word walks
Through meridians,
Mistakes,
Archives.
But it needs
A translation
Walking on stilts
To cross
Its own body.
The word walks
Through melancholies,
Advertisements,
Concepts.
Sometimes it's a horse.
It wanders into a gap.
While walking,
Tired of the blah blah,
It silently, silently
Falls asleep.

The word YET.
A word that
Requests
Approval.
You nod.
The word YET.
It quenches none
Of the thirst,
Extinguishes none
Of the demand
That simultaneously
Fills up everything.
The word YET.
A word
Of time
In time.
A word
That requests
A minute
Without thirst,
An incident
That extinguishes
The eye.
And yet
In the eye
There is a desert,
And in the desert
A camel
That crosses
This poem.
The pressure of thirst
Leads it over
The path
Of this transcription.
The word YET.
A word that
Requests.
An oasis,

But this poem
Doesn't know
About the oasis.
Thirsty, it drinks,
Is even more
Thirsty.
Thirsty, it searches
In circles,
Wringing itself out.
Inside its
Hump
It carries
What it
Thirsts for.
Where,
And what kind,
And whose
Time
Does it carry?
And who
Is the small
Sultan
Who sits
With a halter
Between his teeth,
Murmuring
Further, further?

FROM

Above the Sky Beneath the Earth

(2015)

The Boy

Here comes the boy who plays
On a halogen light.
Because of the noise
Nothing can be seen.
In fetid cellars he leaves behind
Plasters and fish oil.
This is not a metaphysical era.
This is not an era for the voice.
This is the era of halogenic noise.
Unplug the herring from your ears.
Can you smell my fear?
The forecast sets
In a broken puddle.
Our era began
Like a toothache.
It will end with the hallucinations
Of microbes in the dark.

Gnashing Teeth

Esteemed doctor of culture!
Birds fly beneath the roots.
Computers are sweating.
At the poles, holes grow,
And deaf-mute people rush
From inside them
To scrape the sclera
And shame from our eyes.
Our names are proteins.
We are happy when we burn them.
Cherished doctor,
Internationally ill expert
On the manufacture of souls.
Without a doubt we are dialogic.
Whoever doubts goes in the pit,
Whoever doesn't doubt goes the only way.
No doctrines. The time of salvation is already
Breathing down a dirty neck.
The day arrives like a poem
In a lost language.
A barefoot girl is pricked
By a forgotten word
And gnashes her teeth.

The Revolt Against the End of Summer

He writes, places marks, becomes excited,
Wastes his whole life on an apparently useless activity.

No one notices his undertaking.
Children run around, unaware they erase his efforts.

Despite everything, he's convinced that the fate of the universe
Is in his hands, depends on his persistence.

What was uncovered countless times
Will be uncovered again.

His activity prolongs the word *foam*,
The word *fan*, the word *this*, the word *presence*.

It prolongs the artful veiling
That accompanies the seducer, poetry.

Weary bathers shake the towels
They were lying on all day on the sand.

What remains is an impression that will be erased again and again.
What there is is the revolt against the end of summer.

Time Is

Time is a migratory bird.
Man has
The genome of a stone.

Man and Truth

Between truth and man
I choose waiting.

Between waiting and man
I choose plastic flowers.

I am not foolish,
Wanting to be a genius.

All I want is
The stiff penises of meteorologists.

May they forecast precisely,
Preventing the slaughter of my Isaac.

WWW

The master's spiders are weaving
A wireless network around us.

Someone on another continent
Secretly reads our thoughts.

Through the door nothing is visible.
In the dark we are smaller than gnats.

My palms reach for you,
Sink into a veiled mirror.

When I finally reach you,
I embrace the whole world.

Olympics

If a great idea is translated into a body,
Then Greg Louganis is an Einstein.

If a body is translated into a great idea,
Einstein is *tralala oompah*.

Which gods do chess grandmasters dream about?

It is time, my love, that we all participate
In this outrageous activity.

Let bankers with pacemakers run the marathon.
Let naked sumo wrestlers decide our common fate.

Let us pierce the concrete with our heads.

Every time it's a top score
And we are in no hurry to get anywhere.

O E

The Lord said Mountain.
Snow fell and covered the Lord.

The Lord called Spring
And it came running out of the mountain.

The Lord disappeared into the tops of pines.
Summer blazed on the surface of the lake.

The Lord watched a man
Who bathed himself in the Lord.

O   E
Murmured the Lord.

How much of the Lord has to pass by
So that one solemn man becomes purified.

My Body Is a Central Committee

My body is a Central Committee.
The blood is the Party's cell for religious and ideological questions.
You dream too materialistically,
My Komsomol comrades tease me.
In order to be better, I grab my soul
And hurl it over the threshold.
Let it disappear until the next Congress, only so there's peace.
But soon it flutters back, wanders around,
Knocks over chairs and leafs through the books of my Chinese comrades.
It would like to be one of them and die smoothly.
Thus I must deal with
Destroying the intangible plot of our future.
In the next life I will choose other ancestors,
A more courteous environment, feed on roots,
Die like a stone on the grate of a hydroelectric plant.
But as a European I hang onto my soul
Like mass killings hang on the testicles of revolution.
The soul returns from church. Says that the flame of the funeral candle is
        beautiful.
I hurl it into the crematory. Scorch its wings.
It returns shaken up, shouts that fire is a dreadful class enemy.
I hurl it into the last circle of hell.
From there it communicates no signs.
What good practice and eons teach:
1. The Party must adopt
An eternal moratorium on the souls of the dead returning.
2. The Party must reward
Self-immolation and other bodily pleasures.
3. The Party must become mystical
Towards death, like my name is in relation
To cells, from which it disappears
Without ever living in them.

Erasure of Possibilities

A person isn't a spot.
A person is a tail.
In absolute reality
All scenarios
Are possible.
Our spectrum
Is the strait.
We are all,
But at the same time
All possibilities
Aren't for us.
Oh, my lovely blinders!
Oh, my gorgeous tail!
Oh, the past,
Which sits on me like
A fly on a nose.
Fate gives us
Unbearable freedom.
That's why I'd rather
Pull and pull
The whole world like a puzzle
That I created.
No, a person isn't a spot.
Truth isn't a horse.
I affirm this, unshod
And under no duress.

Magic Square

At the circus I got
A magic square.
Nine symbols.
Their sum always death.

Mother sent me
To your unknown
Residence
For a reading.

Before I even learned
Where to search,
I became the shape
Of your absence.

The Whole World Is a Uterus

The umbilical cord still hangs
Between the abandoned telegraph poles.
The whole world is a uterus.
The living and the dead send
Wireless messages.

My Mother

My mother
Who art in bodies,
Devastation is your name.
Come to me at least
In your exile,
Your brutality occurs
In poverty and plenty.
Toss today at least
A worthless crumb
And forgive me
My moments of weakness,
When I try to steal more from life
Than you intend.
Don't lead me once more into emptiness,
May my bones be crushed
When you caress me,
Mother.

Permanently on Loan

A poet is born
When she hears a voice.

The voice is immortal.
It is here. Permanently
On loan.

For a moment the chirping of a blackbird
Drowns out the roar of the crowd.

Love is an unstitched thread.
The textile industry is sacred.

Where did you hear this?
In my ear.

The World Is Without Culprits

Father is the outcome of my words.
He grows in test tubes and clouds.
The door of guilt and a private curse.
I tell him: up yours.
He goes, peers out through a mouth.
Life is an ellipse and an oxymoron.
It has no more than five words.
First: love is the indifference of meteorology.
There's nothing wrong with rain.
Second: the world is without culprits.
My stammering spells the periodic table.
Third: to be free on the farm of the gods.
Happiness is when I shovel.
Fourth: I'm always repeating my father again.
He grows like cavities and architecture.
Fifth: there is no justice, only revolution.
The oxymoron is life in an ellipse.
It has no more than five words.
The sixth sticks deep in the throat.
And the seventh is, reportedly, indigestible and silent.
The elliptical oxymoron of life.

Sweet Snow

From palms
Bloody from
St John's wort
And drunken grapes
I received the news
That everything is related
And is simultaneously
Good and evil.

Woe is me.
What does clay turn into,
What does breath,
When will sweet snow
Cover me?

The Sky

The sun is stuck
In the crown of a century-old oak.

If only I too could
Recline always awake

In its clear shadow,
The sky in my eyes.

White Shirt

I have a white shirt.
In the middle of the night
A dark body glows in it.

White is the border.
I live here.
I am spoken there.

I have a white,
Snowy,
Angelic shirt.

I raise the collar.
Unfasten a button.
Roll up a sleeve.

Language gets dirty.
The angel gets dirty.
The soul gets dirty.

But I still live
In my snowy clean,
In my perfectly white shirt.

Elementary Laws

Reason has a wish
But cannot control
My destiny.

The soul can control
Destiny,
But it has no will.

I tuck reason
Into a black briefcase
And my soul behind an ear.

As I walk alone
The black briefcase rattles.
Someone is whispering to me.

Lindens in the Desert Sand

I did not throw myself into the crater of Mount Etna
Or into the voracious mouth of Pantagruel.

I planted lindens in the desert sand. Dug graves in silence.
Nothing grew. No one echoed.

The sight of silent oracles and fog dealers
Fed me bitter honey when I was weak.

I did not regret. I am a decaying descent
In the direction of an opaque reflection. Whose, I don't know.

When we meet, the sound of the sea will be my pillow,
The shadow of a seagull on my eyelid.

I Feel Everything

According to esoteric theories
The human aura is infinite,
Though increasingly diluted with distance.

I just brushed against someone
On the other side of the universe.
And on the contrary, I'm touching everything.

How many encounters, how much inevitability!
It's good that my mind is limited
And my name is untranslatable.

Behind a Curtain

Sometimes it grows dark on earth.
Your home deep in dusk.
Behind a window curtain, like a mirage,
A tiny light in the dark.

Whoever thinks *hope* misses it.
It flickers so that you sense your shadow,
A blind Tiresias who soaks his fingers
In the blackness of letters. Feels the cracks. Follows.

No One

When I speak, I give birth to chaos.
It climbs from my mouth.
Words only conceal it temporarily.
The gust of time blows them away.
Chaos stands up and grows.
May my eye not close
When my Polyphemus swallows me.

A Place

There's a place in you
Where you secretly live,
Forbidden shards,
A place where
No one may go.

Nothing sweeter
Than being
A passing doe
Licking this place
With a bleeding tongue.

Above the Sky Beneath the Earth

Shall I fall into the grey sky,
Into the pale stroke in the grey,

Into the trace that, behind a feeling, reveals
That it does not exist, and thus will return.

Shall I fall, vanish into the in-between
Like a mouse into the night flour, sleepless?

And never awaken except in letters.
Shall I fall and fall and leave

Because I love returning, because I am
Above the sky, beneath the earth, forever.

Five Assertions

Five assertions,
This is all
The years have washed up.

First: I loved you
Even before I existed.

Second: my life
Is a drop of black ink in the boundless night.

Third: There is no end,
Only snow-covered mountain peaks.

Fourth: The sea doesn't
Care about us.

Last: There is no end,
Only glaciers are dying.

Testimony

(2020)

You ask me

You ask me, *what is humility?*

I meet you, who's reading this,
As an equal.

At the same time, I am humbled before
The infinite in you.

It's possible to read the signs
In more ways than there are souls.

But love is one. And one is knowledge.
And one is you. And one I.

And the sum of you and I is one.

Ancestors

We went to the village cemetery.
In Destrnik the cemetery is the only place
Open on all four sides of the sky.
There, one across from the other,
Like a mirror looking into a mirror,
Lie the grave of my mother's family
And the grave of my father's family.
We carried neither ashes nor bones.
I suddenly understood why cemeteries
Were important and to whom I whispered there.
That we are only a part of everything.
We went to the village cemetery and wept,
But we did not weep from sorrow.
In the spacious cellar of the Scheinburg castle,
Among the bricks with centuries-old histories,
I was also in Destrnik at the village cemetery,
Open on all four sides of the sky.
I entered each of them,
Which gave birth to me even before I was conceived.
Four sides of the sky, four ancestors,
Four souls required for me to be here.
I travelled north.
My grandmother Vida stands there. Pura vida.
Born in Paradise.
A woman without an embrace, without touch.
The most beautiful voice at the church of St Urban.
A small, poor child from Haloze
Who loved a lost love her entire life
And only befriended my grandfather
As much as it was possible.
Although everything is possible.
Even healing the past.
My grandmother Vida. Pura Vida.
With so much unlived inside her,
With so much buried in her soul of clay,

Who gave me incessant restlessness
And efficiency, incessant drive
And the inexhaustible power to go on,
To reinvent myself again and again.
I travelled south.
To the warm south, where tenderness and mercy
Drift from the crowns of chestnuts.
But this too is a singular strategy,
How to traffic in tears and emotions,
In resentment and acceptance.
My grandmother Kristina,
A miracle of survival and devotion,
A soft palm that caressed me
And protected me despite all that may come.
Grandmother Kristina, who as a child
Found her father hanged
And all her life prayed a rosary
That never ends.
I travelled west.
There my second father, my grandfather Matijas,
Welcomed me with a smile.
Matijas, with hands white from baker's flour,
Matijas, who taught me to read what's concealed,
The Nazi's and the Partisan's secrets, who taught me
The words *Gott, Schoß, Teufel*
So that I recognise them now on signs
Around the castle, where I breathe, where with each breath
I enter into him, into his suspenders
And books, into his stories about good and evil.
Always without a name. Always without names.
Is the beginning of poetry here, in the secret
Of a language without names?
I travelled east,
To the most untameable, most thoughtful
And least articulate of the four.
My grandfather Ignac, a stranger,
Whom I resemble the most.
Words were good only

If they were defeated,
If they were released like the animals
In his stable, like the cats and birds
He shared his solitude with.
Open on four sides of the sky,
Among Vida, Kristina, Matijas, and Ignac,
I travelled through the most precious,
Through the moments that shaped me,
Through my light, infinite light,
Undeferrable luggage,
Above us my mother the sky,
Beneath us my father the earth.
I opened my eyes.
In a corner of the castle cellar were two shamans,
Gaya and Quil smoking tobacco
And observing how the message
Older than man shaped us.
In the middle of the room a fire flickered.
Dizzy, I moved
Closer to it.
Fire, fire, fire which burns
Our bones and flesh to ash.
For a long time I stared at the dancing flames.
I deeply inhaled my north, my south,
I inhaled east and west.
Carry me to where I belong, I begged them,
Carry me to where I have always lived,
But without a voice and without words,
Where I'll live like the stones and trees live,
Like the changing faces of clouds.
Then I felt how
From my head a second head grew,
A head of light and pain,
An unrecognisable head of an angelic monster,
It bent before me and entered
Me again between my legs,
Pierced my body,
And then two more heads appeared.

An intoxicating, invigorating circulation.
I felt the fourth head grow,
Vertebra by vertebra,
All space suddenly vanished.
It was the time of my ancestors,
Who circulated through me,
It was north in every direction,
And south, and east, and west.
I looked at my body.
It was no more.
There were my mother and father,
Embracing, the tightly closed nakedness of conception.
I was no more.
Instead of me there was only
The bare time of circulation.
And then out of my head stepped
My sister, my wife, my son,
More and more people like tiny beams of light
Whose presence I carried inside me.
It started to rain.
The fire grew stronger,
Increasingly gentle and clear and mild.
I became the source of everything I am,
And everything I am constantly spilled out of me
And returned again and again.
Time without time.
I saw a planet
From which the souls of the dead fly
And return,
Without shape, silent and purified
By the single light of love,
By a single lamp,
By the single flame
Of a dark candle that never goes out
In the village cemetery.

Between this

Between this, what you call a dream,
And this, what you call wakefulness,
There is a liquid edge,
A grey zone,
Two colours blending.
Gently. Gently.
The massive walls of the castle fortress
(The walls of the castle where I am are eight metres wide)
Are here so I can freely
Step through them.
Gently. Gently.

On a plate

On a plate in the hotel restaurant
There are grains of white rice and a few tomato slices.

On a plate in the hotel restaurant
There are the hands that planted the rice, bent backs in the burning sun
And bare feet sunk in the mud of rice fields.

On a plate in the hotel restaurant
There are grains of white light that tell us
It's a gift not to be hungry.

On a plate in the hotel restaurant
There are the glowing fruits of a plant that is given for us.

So many tiny red-hot suns on a plate
In a hotel restaurant that was built
By our ancestors' hands, our ancestors' tongues, our ancestors' dreams.

The tomato slices are their cut-up hearts.
How sweetly, how uniquely they beat
In the late evening light.

Ant

You see an ant carrying a dead ant.
Only together do they make what you call life.
You're alive only as much as you're already dead.
But not living dead. Revived by death.
By everything you've been.
By everything you've fled.
The pure motionlessness of motion.
A dead ant moving a living one.

The world will return

The world will return,
They'll return, the familiar streets
And heaps of obligations.

The wish will return
To be more successful in the beautiful lie
That we try to build day after day.

The world will return,
They'll return, the vendors of ice cream
And other things that have no end.

Rain teaches us

Rain teaches us:
Don't search, place yourself in the rain.

It teaches us, rain, how to scatter
The clouds inside us.
For whom does it rain from a clear sky?

Rain tells us:
Every correction is a detour.
They are only approximations of large storms.

It secretly confided in me:
For others, I will fall all night,
For you only, your entire life.

When someone asks

When someone asks *How are you?*
Don't answer: *I am fine.*
Answer: *I'm searching.*
No more hollow words.
How are you?
A crystal clear sky. That's how I am.

New Poems

In the children's hospital

Then I knew it was my task
To carry the sky with my breath and to cure distances.

The scent of cafeteria and disinfectant
Emitted toxic bubbles into my play.

I had sowed wind and clouds and hugs at such a density
That my thoughts were about to explode due to the sweet scent of freedom.

To breathe. Not to breathe. It was a crafty solution.
It was everything. But not in human words. Not yet.

Everything was disappearing. Turning off the light. Emptying spring.
The breathing machine demanded that I still go on.

It said that other mute things also exist.
It said that humans also breathe after they die.

I breathed in the whispers of gods and breathed out the screaming of people.
It felt good to share with loved ones the inhalation and the exhalation.

I was the inhalation and the exhalation, and with me
Were a wheelchair and a cloud and a syringe.

I called beyond the words and you came,
Father Ether and mother Rhea, father Science and mother Luna.

I lay my tired head in your arms
Like a sunflower in a poor farmer's hands.

Inhale, father, all that is mine.
Exhale, mother, all that is inevitable.

Inhale, father, your creation is white and terrifying.
Exhale, mother, you who are everywhere except with me.

Then I knew that my task was completed.
Like the drowned I was carried deeper into the indifference of words.

My dear father

My dear father, you know that I know
What my small son knows, that nothing remains,
Not the word, not the body.

In your body lives the memory of the corpse of your father,
Who could not forget the childhood scene with the worms
That crawled out of the skull of his father.

I look at you, your head in bandages, on a hospital bed,
And I know, my dear father, that it is in vain, all in vain,
Nothing remains, neither the word nor the body.

Skin rots, organs liquefy,
Tissue and muscles become compost,
And soon the bones are only dust.

You are the son of my memory, father, I am the last witness
Of your father, my son is the underwriter of your decay,
Which will last as long as a man who remembers it will live.

Thus bodies and words go into nothingness.
All effort in vain. Paltry. And all this grotesque
Exertion of ours to last a brief moment longer.

Yesterday they operated on you, concealed a dead screw
In your broken jaw, a worm made of titanium
That one day will testify as the only survivor

Of the vanished son and the vanished lineage
And the vanished place where, dear father,
Forgotten words and bodies once met

In perdition.

My little god

At birth
A little god
Hid inside me.

I change,
He is always
Only himself.

We don't totally overlap.
I often call him,
He isn't there.

Sometimes he reaches out of me
And strokes others' gods
Without me noticing.

He isn't bad, my little god,
Just misunderstood and alone.
I pity him.

I wouldn't want to be in his skin.
But he is in mine,
So I am grateful to him.

Only tonight

Only tonight is there life.
Tonight I died again.

I died again tonight
And I know it's not the last time.

I know it's not the last time
My small wide death.

My multiple small death
Is a dandelion puff.

Like a light in the voice of the wind, I go,
I go so that I will die on all sides.

On all sides there is life tonight.
But I'm nowhere tonight.

Mountain

This mountain does and does not have a name.
It has a name that persistently evades.

Not a name, only a mute crease
Of yet another everyday loss.

In vain you address the clearing of pines,
In vain the black stomachs of clouds.

The name of the mountain persistently evades,
Teaches you, without purpose, without cause,

To seek, to call, to shout,
To despair, to toy with despair.

Mountain mountain mountain in front of me.
Scree scree scree inside.

Inside, where there are many broken shadows,
A lot of scree but no trees.

From the scree a silent rock grows.
From the silent rock, a solid mountain.

This mountain does and does not have a name.
It has a name that persistently evades.

A mountain mountain mountain in me.
Scree scree scree everywhere.

In front of the border

In front of the border of your kingdom
We have sewn our mouths shut.

You have stored our names in the archives,
Which are gnawed by fish and the wind.

Your most enduring saints succumbed
Beneath the weight of our bones.

In front of the golden doors to your kingdom
We have sewn our names for you into our mouths.

We enter mute, with burning tongues.

From the other side we have silently
And permanently sewn the border into you.

Swimming pool

An ice-blue uterus
Filled with clouds and contrails.

A rippling promise that we all will return
Into amniotic fluid, even if chlorinated.

I accept everything. I renounce everything.
I sink into everything, clothed only in a wet beard.

I float in you like trash, like dead insects,
Like a petrol spill, like lazy sperm

And dream of all the fat, which now dreams
In one of your repetitions the same dream about me.

Seen from the sky you are one of the countless teardrops
Painted on the mask of a murdered demon.

Syracuse

Spellbound by histories.
Athena and the Virgin in one.
The architecture of pain
And the cries of gulls over the shore.

The eye is impartially hungry
For stucco, cherubim, Doric wars,
Ecstatically in time,
Which shields it from the present.

It's a pleasure pleasure pleasure
To stroll around Syracuse
Because once it was Aleppo.

On the screens, rafts. In the water, bodies.
I blindly stare at indifferent stones.
The past is now and here since long ago.

Outside a station of the metro

Fallen ginkgo leaves,
New York, Nazis,
And other still-lifes
From history on a leash.

We are warmed by safe periodic systems,
Congo, the Maccabees, and Rome.
How strange. Our ancestors
Know nothing about our lives.

Fallen ginkgo leaves
Under a million feet.
And Goethe in Guantánamo,
Goethe in Guantánamo.

What are our poets smiling at?

What are our poets smiling at?
There's nothing funny in our tribe.

Many lie murdered in gullies.
Our women and children are hungry and barefoot.

Unknown illnesses are mowing us down.
No new villages built and soon it will snow.

Despite all this, the smiles don't fade from our poets' faces.
As if facing sorrow brings them irrational, secret joy.

When we ask them what's funny, they silently shrug,
And do the same when we demand they cheer us up in these dark times.

They guard the reason for their smiling just for their own enjoyment.
We trust them less and less, believe their sparse words less and less.

The smiles of our poets are truly mysterious in these poor times.
Did their minds burn out? Do they mock our common misery?

Their smiling sometimes cuts more cruelly than the weapons of our enemies.
But they are wrong if they think they will deceive us.

We will kill our poets only when we squeeze their secret out of them.
We will leave alive only the biggest blatherers, sombre-faced and resembling us.

An old poet

An old poet looks back on his life,
Says it was only inevitable to set oneself
In a political sense toward the revolution.

Another day another poet says
I felt an historical necessity to write,
Says it was like it was writing me.

Another poet silently weighs in.
Whatever I said, he says, whatever I wrote,
It was a mistake and silence is my one true home.

Don't speak nonsense, says a poet at night,
We are a function of excess and the infinite,
And as such no better than hamsters in the wheel of language.

I worked to the best of my abilities,
Says a poet on the edge of insanity, groping in the void,
Not knowing where, nor why, again and again.

A little reason doesn't hurt and neither does a little humor,
A poet protests, we must wipe away all this metaphysical junk,
To bite into and get dirty with my era, that was my mission.

A young poet fitfully looks forward on all his wishes.
An old poet condescendingly looks back on all he wrote.
A poet of the middle generation writes, doesn't look.

Pines

Green pine and mute pine
In the middle of a car park.

Two, which are one and none
From the same standpoint.

A greendead living voice
Glows among the twigs.

Like a doubled, secret time
Anchored at the base of things.

On the eve of the future
The last guest drives off.

They were here, are, are not,
One pine mutely warns.

The other, green inside the green,
Disappears more and more.

Dead kitten

Don't dig into stone, boy in blue.
Your tools are blunt and too old for you.

Don't dig a hole into hard dirt, boy in green.
The seed you're burying will never sprout.

Don't close your eyes, boy in red.
Your mother rests among thorns
And your brothers will never wake again.

Many holes are needed, boy in white.
Many persistent boys, like you.

Don't pet the dead kitten, boy in black.
Let it sleep.

The Sun Walks Behind Me

Today is every Monday.
Tonight we'll be on our way again.
I love and am the words
To the sun, which walks, which walks.

Today is every Monday,
Another body goes into the mud.
I am a seed.
The sun walks behind me.

More persistent than dust and weed,
I'm free to disappear into the unknown.
Increasingly quiet, increasingly bold.
The sun walks behind me.

I love you by the light of the night.
I love, for I'm an exile.
I love in complete darkness.
The sun walks behind me.

When grass awakes again
And the river whispers in harmony,
When I, when we are gone,
The sun walks behind me.

Today is every Monday,
Tonight you'll be on your way again.
Go through complete darkness
Towards the sun, which walks, which walks.

What is half an hour

What is half an hour
If everything is halved.
An apple, a life
And the path seen only by you.

Half a little bird flies by
And half a memory
Appears and dissolves
And half a mother and father.

I learned to
Lose and in loss
To call forth the lost
With a blind word.

A poem cannot do any more.
To fall where the power that gradually
Heals its own wound appears.
Do you know it, love?

The Autobiography of H

a

I saw a human
Kill a human
With a word.

b

A human is a hunt.
A human is a voice.
A human is two.
A human is a mensch.
A human is a human who doesn't know how to know
What all may be,
What all may become
Human.

c

Human
Goes to non-human
And back.

Chasms, monsters, trials.

The place where his trace is lost
Lends him a name.

č

Human č.
That's what they called him.
Better that than human number.
Human č is satisfied č.

d

A human rarely flies,
A human more often hunts
Flying people.

If a human isn't free,
If he doesn't know what the sky is,
He's easily trapped
In the promise of freedom.

e

A human is a shadow
Thrown by a letter.
The letter goes everywhere.
The shadow doesn't leave
The cave.

f

Behind the still fresh ruins of the capitals
And under the ancient script of the first lichens
Is a drop of human blood.

g

Conceived from the collision of two thoughts:
A human doesn't want to be a human.
A human loves kills
Water ferns humans.

h

A human is a tear.
A human is a stone.
The ocean wakes him up,
Tosses him around,
A human is less
Than human sand.

i

A human fearfully protects
His mysterious self Self SELF.
The self is a closed stone eye.
If a human's eye opened,
He would fall through it among the stars.
An ecstatic human.
A terrified human.

j

A human is no builder.
No no, at no time in
No name a human
Is not no a human is not at home.

k

Ridicule
Self-destruction
The magic of inadequate miracles.
Human god human.

l

Milk turns to ash.
History to oblivion.
A deer eats a weed
In the garden
Of the dead mother
Of another human.

m

Death is a craft
And the days are doomed.
Despite everything,
A human opens his arms

Ready once again
To try.
To try.

n

A human is not.
A human is.
How much clever nonsense
To make a human think not think
He did not live
On and on.

o

There is a crack
In everything (even in this quotation).
A human hopes
To slip through it one day,
Leave the human.

þ

A human kisses the sky,
Blesses the water,
Goes through the earth.
There is no end no peace
No human
For the human.

r

Can a human be r?
A human cannot not be a rupture.
But r?
A black crow carries r
Into the black sky.
But who carries away the human?
Revolution. Rut. Republic.

s

The soil begins at s.
Something is spawned, it slithers,
Becomes spiteful and secret.
The human loves something.
The human can't manage without something.

š

I bear the unspeakable.
I'm human.
But what for?
But why?

t

My comrade on the cross,
How I would love
To free you of thoughts of limbs,
Turn you into a pool,
Into a milky carousel
Of the perfect human.

u

War alphabets formed him.
He's a lover of perfect systems,
This opportunistic human of ours.

v

At last I saw you, despite everything,
Accepted you (not without resistance).

If I didn't, I'd still be human,
Staromil, Bogomil, Chernobyl human.

So now I'm a human who isn't human,
Only when abandoned am I truly human.

z

Between human and human
There is no difference, just a pause and pain.

Only in the gap where the human ends up
Is the birth of a human possible.

ž

The only thing
That a human
Nowhere never
No no, he doesn't understand,
The only thing is not
The end the beginning
The beginning the end of the human.

NOTES

'**Urinal**' [43]: Fa is a popular brand of soap in Europe. Faronika is a mythological fish common in old Slovenian folk songs. Faronika carries the world on its back, and when there is too much evil in the world, Faronika will dive into the cosmic sea and thus destroy the world.

'**Knives**' [53]: The population of Slovenia is two million. After World War II, the Communists killed 15,000 Slovenians, who'd been stopped in Austria by British troops and returned to Tito's partisans.

'**Jelly**' [54]:Tivoli is the main park in Ljubljana, Slovenia. Cf. Jakob von Hoddis' 'Weltende'.

'**Mint**' [56]: In Slovenian, 'meta' means 'mint'. The poem plays on the correspondence between 'mint' and the prefix 'meta'.

'**Saliva**' [59]: Cf. T.S. Eliot's 'Fragment of an Agon'.

'**Hayrack**' [63]: King Matjaž is a figure in Slovenian mythology (derived from the Hungarian king Matthias Corvinus, 1458-1490) who sleeps with his army hidden in the Peca mountain, destined to awake and liberate his country. 'The land' in the poem ('dežela') is also a pejorative term for Slovenia due to a 1980s-era promotion slogan for the country: 'Dobrodošli v deželi'. The hayrack is a common Slovenian tourist symbol. '[M]orphield' is a neologism corresponding with the neologism 'travmal' in the original text; 'travmal' combines the Slovenian word for 'grass' with the name of a popular analgesic (Tramal). The military figures near the end of the poem are imaginary colonels from the four countries that border Slovenia – Italy, Austria, Hungary, Croatia.

'**Salmon**' [67]: Destrnik is a small village in eastern Slovenia.

'**The closer the deadline**' [112]: Cf. Tomaž Šalamun's 'Jonah'.

ACKNOWLEDGEMENTS

Three of Aleš Šteger's poetry books have been fully translated into English and published in the US: *The Book of Things* (BOA Editions, 2010), *Above the Sky Beneath the Earth* (White Pine Press, 2019) and *The Book of Bodies* (White Pine Press, 2022). Thanks to the publishers for permission to reprint poems from those books here, and particular thanks to Peter Conners at BOA for ushering Šteger's first English-language book into print, and to Dennis Mahoney at White Pine for his subsequent support. Also thanks to Rod Mengham at Equipage and Dara Wier at Factory Hollow Press for publishing chapbooks including some of these poems.

Many of these translations first appeared in *Almost Island, Asymptote, Beltway Poetry Quarterly, Bennington Review, Blackbird, Bomb, Boston Review, The Brooklyn Rail, Chicago Review, Cincinnati Review, Circumference, Colorado Review, Columbia Journal, Conduit, Conjunctions, Copper Nickel, Crazyhorse, Denver Quarterly, Eleven Eleven, Field, Guernica, Gulf Coast, jubilat, Laurel Review, Manoa: A Pacific Journal of International Writing, Modern Poetry in Translation, New American Writing, New England Review, The New Humanist, The New Yorker, Ninth Letter, North American Review,* NPR's *Morning Edition, Parthenon West Review, Ping Pong, Poetry in Action, Poetry International, Poetry London, Poetry Review, A Public Space, Redivider, The Rupture, Solstice, The Southern Review, Subtropics, Trafika Europe, TriQuarterly, Tupelo Quarterly, Virginia Quarterly Review, Volt, Washington Square, West Branch* and *Zoland Poetry*. Thanks to the editors for their support.

The Book of Things received the 2011 Best Translated Book Award for Poetry and the 2011 Best Literary Translation Award from AATSEEL.

This project is supported in part by an award from the National Endowment for the Arts.

Brian Henry is the author of eleven books of poetry, most recently *Permanent State* (Threadsuns, 2020) and the prose book *Things Are Completely Simple: Poetry and Translation* (Parlor, 2022). Three of his books (*Astronaut*, *Graft* and *Quarantine*) have appeared in separate UK editions from Arc Publications. He co-edited the international magazine *Verse* from 1995 to 2018 and established the Tomaž Šalamun Prize in 2015. His translation of Aleš Šteger's *The Book of Things* appeared from BOA Editions in the US in 2015 and won the Best Translated Book Award. He also has translated Tomaž Šalamun's *Woods and Chalices* (Harcourt, 2008), Aleš Debeljak's *Smugglers* (BOA Editions, 2015), and Aleš Šteger's *Berlin* (Counterpath, 2015), *Above the Sky Beneath the Earth* (White Pine, 2019), *The Book of Bodies* (White Pine, 2022) and *Burning Tongues: New & Selected Poems* (Bloodaxe Books, 2022). His poetry and translations have received numerous honours, including two NEA fellowships, a Howard Foundation grant, the Alice Fay di Castagnola Award, the Carole Weinstein Poetry Prize, the Cecil B. Hemley Memorial Award, the George Bogin Memorial Award, and a Slovenian Academy of Arts and Sciences grant.